STECK–VAUGHN

# PREPARATION
## FOR
# CITIZENSHIP

Steck Vaughn

HOUGHTON MIFFLIN HARCOURT
Supplemental Publishers

www.SteckVaughn.com
800-531-5015

## Photography and Art Credits

ISBN 13:  978-1-4190-5333-7
ISBN 10:     1-4190-5333-7

# CONTENTS

# To the Learner

Congratulations! You are on your way to becoming a U.S. citizen. *Preparation for Citizenship* will help you get ready for the United States Citizenship and Immigration Services (USCIS) naturalization test and interview. When you finish this book, you will be able to answer questions about the history of the United States. You will understand how the U.S. government works. In addition, you will learn other important facts about life in the United States.

At your USCIS interview, you will need to show that you know English. As you study the lessons, you will get practice speaking, reading, and writing English. You will also have a chance to practice listening to and speaking with your classmates and your teacher.

We hope you enjoy learning about your new country.

Good luck!

# TO THE INSTRUCTOR

*Preparation for Citizenship* is designed for non-native speakers of English who are applicants for naturalization and want to prepare for the civics and English test and interview required by U.S. Citizenship and Immigration Services (USCIS). *Preparation for Citizenship* features simple English and a variety of visual aids that highlight and clarify important facts and concepts. The program is suitable for English as a Second Language learners at beginning through low-intermediate levels.

The instructional material in *Preparation for Citizenship* is based on the questions and answers on U.S. history and government provided by USCIS. Each lesson focuses on a key topic, and the instructional sequence is designed to help learners master new vocabulary and sentence patterns at the same time that they are learning new information. The accompanying CD focuses on the information learners will need in order to succed during the USCIS test and interview.

## TO THE LEARNER

The first time you present the program to learners, you may wish to read the *To the Learner* section with the class. Point out that English language skills are an important part of the USCIS test and interview process and explain that the *Preparation for Citizenship* book and CD will give them confidence with this process.

## UNIT OVERVIEW

*Preparation for Citizenship* is divided into three units: U.S. History, U.S. Government, and Integrated Civics.

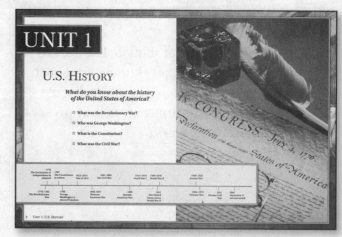

**Unit Opener**   Each unit opener features a photograph, a timeline, and several discussion questions. These elements place the material in context, identify the key content to be covered, and encourage learners to share what they already know about the topic.

The Unit Opener provides a framework for the study of several individual lessons. Begin by having learners look at the featured photo and asking them to tell you what they see. Read the questions aloud and encourage learners to answer as well as they can. This allows them to recognize what they know and builds confidence in their ability to master the material. Invite learners to explain what they think they will learn and encourage them to make up questions of their own. The timeline draws students into the content of the unit. Briefly discuss each item on the timeline, paraphrasing and explaining in simple English as needed. Invite learners to name similar events from the history of their countries.

## ABOUT THE LESSONS

All lessons follow a similar format, including a preview of what students will learn and a vocabulary list, *Words to Know.* This is followed by pages of activities designed to help learners make use of all four language skills to master the content. Each lesson ends with a *Figure It Out* activity. These pages provide a final review as well as an informal assessment of how well learners have mastered the material.

The following is a list of suggestions for how to make use of each segment of a lesson. Before you read further, remember that the key to your learners' success is to get them involved. Adults bring a wealth of information and experience to the learning process. Helping them activate this background information will have a positive effect on their ability to make sense of what they read and hear in class. Comparing and contrasting the history, government, and celebrations of the United States with those of their native countries will open communication and increase their rate of success.

## LESSON OPENER

### CD Icons

The CD icon and track number next to the lesson title identify the corresponding track number on the audio CD. Subsequent CD icons identify which parts of the lesson text are included on the track.

### Preview

Read the list aloud and invite learners to share what they already know about each item. You can also have learners discuss the list in small groups before they present their ideas to the class.

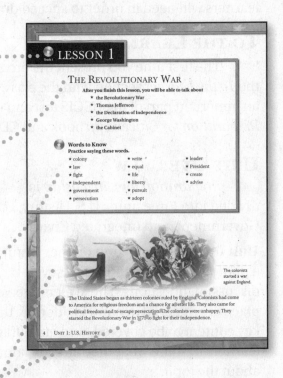

### Words to Know

The words on this list are presented in the order in which they appear in the lesson. In most cases, only the base form of the word appears. Read each word aloud and have learners pronounce it several times. Then invite learners to explain the meanings of the words they already know and use each one in a sentence. Define any unfamiliar terms in simple English. Use pictures or sample sentences to clarify the meaning. Use a bilingual dictionary if appropriate.

### Pictures and Captions

Every lesson includes multiple photographs and paintings with captions that describe the picture. As you begin each lesson, have learners preview the pictures and speculate about what they are going to learn. Later, as learners work with individual pages, point out the pictures again. Read the captions together and discuss how the pictures relate to what they are learning.

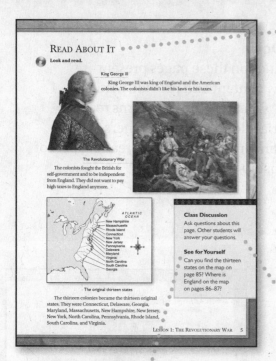

## Read About It

Have learners read each section silently before you read it aloud, play the CD, or have a student read it to the class. Then talk about it with the class. Learners may want to ask questions or discuss vocabulary words from the reading. Then ask some simple factual questions to review the content. Most pages have an additional teaching suggestion at the bottom—*See for Yourself, Partner Work, Group Work,* or *Class Discussion.* All of them encourage learners to learn from each other, extend their productive use of English, reinforce concepts and vocabulary, and prepare for the USCIS test and interview.

## See for Yourself

Have pairs of learners identify or place various geographical locations on the U.S. and world maps on pages 84–87. Encourage them to share their work with other pairs or with the whole class.

## Class Discussion

Have learners write their questions before they present them to the class. Encourage several learners to respond to each question, giving additional information as appropriate.

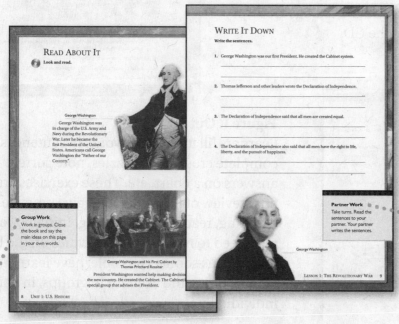

## Group Work

Have learners do this activity in groups of three or four. You may wish to appoint a leader for each group. This person keeps his or her book open and provides language support to the other learners as needed.

## Partner Work

Have pairs of learners review the page. By reading aloud and writing dictated sentences, they prepare for the dictation or reading section of the citizenship test.

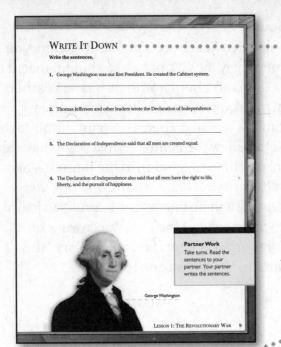

Write the sentences.

1. George Washington was our first President. He created the Cabinet system.

2. Thomas Jefferson and other leaders wrote the Declaration of Independence.

3. The Declaration of Independence said that all men are created equal.

4. The Declaration of Independence also said that all men have the right to life, liberty, and the pursuit of happiness.

**Partner Work**
Take turns. Read the sentences to your partner. Your partner writes the sentences.

George Washington

LESSON 1: THE REVOLUTIONARY WAR     9

## Write It Down

The activities on these pages present and review content and provide writing practice. Ask learners to take turns reading this material aloud to their partners as preparation for the dictation or reading part of the citizenship test.

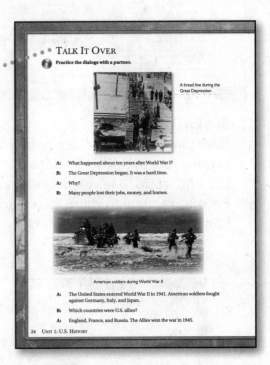

TALK IT OVER
Practice the dialogs with a partner.

A bread line during the Great Depression

A: What happened about ten years after World War I?
B: The Great Depression began. It was a hard time.
A: Why?
B: Many people lost their jobs, money, and homes.

American soldiers during World War II

A: The United States entered World War II in 1941. American soldiers fought against Germany, Italy, and Japan.
B: Which countries were U.S. allies?
A: England, France, and Russia. The Allies won the war in 1945.

24     UNIT 1: U.S. HISTORY

## Talk It Over

*Talk It Over* introduces and reinforce the vocabulary and concepts in each lesson. Since these dialogs are good opportunities for learners to develop their listening and speaking skills, they also provide valuable preparation for the USCIS interview. Read the dialogs aloud or have learners listen to the CD.

FIGURE IT OUT • • • • • • • • • • •
Complete the dialogs. Use the words from the boxes.

George Washington
Father
Revolutionary War
colonies
President
England
Thomas Jefferson
Independence
equal
Declaration

A: In the _____
Americans fought against England.

B: That's right. At that time there were thirteen American _____

A: _____ was in charge of the U.S. military.

B: He was also our first _____

A: That's why we call him the "_____ of our Country."

A: What was the Declaration of _____?

B: It said the colonies were independent from _____

A: Who was the main writer of the _____ of Independence?

B: _____ He wrote that all men are created _____

Practice the dialogs with a partner.

10     UNIT 1: U.S. HISTORY

## Figure It Out

Learners fill in missing words in sentences, complete crossword puzzles, note correct answers on a chart, etc. These exercises are a final review of the lesson and give practice with speaking, reading, and writing. Initially, you may need to model these activities on the board; however, as soon as possible, have learners take charge, doing the exercise in groups, in pairs, or individually.

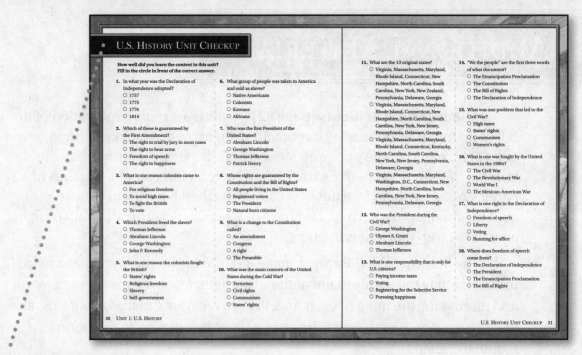

## Unit Checkup

Each unit concludes with a *Checkup* that lets you and your learners assess how well they have mastered the material in the unit. These pages provide test-taking practice with the multiple-choice question.

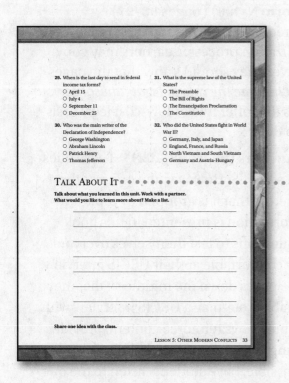

## Talk About It

*Talk About It,* at the end of the *Checkup,* is an opportunity for self-assessment and individual goal-setting.

**About The Bill of Rights (page 82)**    This is a simple explanation of the Bill of Rights. After discussing its content with learners, you may wish to have pairs of learners cut the page into ten sections. Suggest that they write the number of the amendment on the back of each section, shuffle the slips of paper, and place them face down on the desk. Then have them choose a slip, read the number to a partner, and have that person describe the right or rights associated with that amendment.

**The Star-Spangled Banner (page 83)**    Many learners will need help understanding the words to the national anthem. Make a copy for each learner and discuss the meaning of each line. Bring a recording to class for a sing-along or cloze activity. Have learners bring in a recording or sing their country's national anthem.

**United States and World Maps (pages 84–87)**    Use these maps to provide geographical orientation when discussing key events in the United States and around the world. For example, in Lesson 3 have learners find the Confederate states, and in Lesson 4 have them say where they would put the Allied powers.

**Application for Naturalization (Form N-400) (pages 88–97)**
Learners can use this form to review the required information they will have to provide to USCIS as part of the naturalization process. Learners may copy this form and fill it out for practice; however, they should know that the pages have been reduced in size. NOTE: *Do not assume the role of legal advisor to your learners.* Consult with local organizations that offer free or low-cost legal assistance and suggest that learners seek help there.

**NEW Citizenship Questions and Answers (pages 98–102)**    These questions and answers have been provided by a USCIS. However, the order of the questions on this list has been changed so that it is grouped by topic and matches the order in which the information is presented in this book. Encourage learners to use these questions to test themselves over and over so that they feel completely comfortable at their USCIS interview. Model for them how to fold the pages down the middle so that they see only the question. If possible, role-play a USCIS interview with each learner. These mock interviews reinforce content, provide important practice with language skills, and help bolster learners' confidence. Whenever possible, have students listen to the questions on the CD so that they are exposed to a variety of voices.

**Sentences for Dictation and Reading
(pages 103–104)** This is a list of sample sentences for English testing, also provided by USCIS. They are examples of the types of sentences a USCIS officer may ask applicants to read or write during their interview. Since the dictated-sentences part of the citizenship process can be frightening to many learners, you can help by familiarizing them with the process. Dictate or play from the CD two or three sentences during each class period.

**Questions and Answers for the 65/20 Exception
(page 105)** These questions are for applicants who are at least 65 years old and have been living in the United States for at least 20 years. Applicants must answer six of ten questions correctly to pass. They may be tested in the language of their choice. Again, ensure that the learners listen to the questions on the CD to give them experience listening to voices other than yours.

**The Oath of Allegiance (page 106)** Before applicants can become citizens, they must attend a ceremony and take the Oath of Allegiance to the United States. To help prepare learners for what they will have to say at their ceremony, play the CD. Stop and pause at different breaks to allow learners to repeat the oath.

**Answer Key (pages 107–109)** The *Answer Key* contains the answers to all the exercises in the book. Encourage learners to complete each exercise before consulting the answer key.

## CD

The *Preparation for Citizenship* CD contains all of the information presented on the lesson openers, the *Read About It* and *Talk It Over* pages, the *Citizenship Questions and Answers,* the *Sentences for Dictation and Reading,* the *Questions and Answers for the 65/20 Exception,* and the *Oath of Allegiance.* Using the CD helps learners prepare for the citizenship test and interview by exposing them to a variety of native speakers, so encourage learners to use the CD whenever possible. All listening activities are marked with this CD logo.

### HELPFUL WEB SITES

- U.S. Citizenship and Immigration Services
  http://www.uscis.gov
- National Institute for Literacy
  http://www.literacynet.org/esl
- The National Immigration Forum
  http://www.immigrationforum.org
- American Civil Liberties Union
  http://www.aclu.org/immigrants

# UNIT 1

## U.S. HISTORY

### *What do you know about the history of the United States of America?*

☆ **What was the Revolutionary War?**

☆ **Who was George Washington?**

☆ **What is the Constitution?**

☆ **What was the Civil War?**

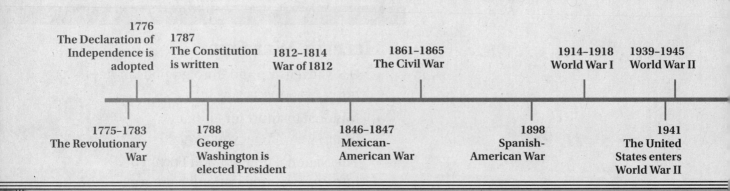

**1776**
The Declaration of Independence is adopted

**1787**
The Constitution is written

**1812–1814**
War of 1812

**1861–1865**
The Civil War

**1914–1918**
World War I

**1939–1945**
World War II

**1775–1783**
The Revolutionary War

**1788**
George Washington is elected President

**1846–1847**
Mexican-American War

**1898**
Spanish-American War

**1941**
The United States enters World War II

IN CONGRESS, JULY 4, 1776.

Declaration of the thirteen united States of America

| 1950–1953 | | | |
| Korean War | | | |
| 1962–1973 | 1991 | 2001 | |
| Vietnam War | Persian Gulf War | September 11 terrorist attack | |

# LESSON 1

# THE REVOLUTIONARY WAR

**After you finish this lesson, you will be able to talk about**

- ★ the Revolutionary War
- ★ Thomas Jefferson
- ★ the Declaration of Independence
- ★ George Washington
- ★ the Cabinet

## Words to Know
**Practice saying these words.**

| | | |
|---|---|---|
| ★ colony | ★ write | ★ leader |
| ★ law | ★ equal | ★ President |
| ★ fight | ★ life | ★ create |
| ★ independent | ★ liberty | ★ advise |
| ★ government | ★ pursuit | |
| ★ persecution | ★ adopt | |

The colonists started a war against England.

The United States began as thirteen colonies ruled by England. Colonists had come to America for religious freedom and a chance for a better life. They also came for political freedom and to escape persecution. The colonists were unhappy. They started the Revolutionary War in 1775 to fight for their independence.

# READ ABOUT IT

 **Look and read.**

King George III
.........................

King George III was king of England and the American colonies. The colonists didn't like his laws or his taxes.

The Revolutionary War
.........................

The colonists fought the British for self-government and to be independent from England. They did not want to pay high taxes to England anymore.

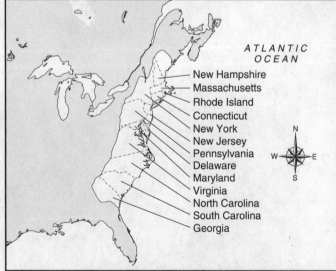

ATLANTIC
OCEAN

New Hampshire
Massachusetts
Rhode Island
Connecticut
New York
New Jersey
Pennsylvania
Delaware
Maryland
Virginia
North Carolina
South Carolina
Georgia

N
W E
S

The original thirteen states

The thirteen colonies became the thirteen original states. They were Connecticut, Delaware, Georgia, Maryland, Massachusetts, New Hampshire, New Jersey, New York, North Carolina, Pennsylvania, Rhode Island, South Carolina, and Virginia.

## Class Discussion

Ask questions about this page. Other students will answer your questions.

## See for Yourself

Can you find the thirteen states on the map on page 85? Where is England on the map on pages 86–87?

# READ ABOUT IT

 **Look and read.**

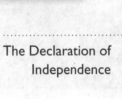

Thomas Jefferson

Thomas Jefferson was the main writer of the Declaration of Independence.

The Declaration of Independence

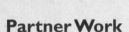

**Partner Work**

Take turns. Read the sentences on this page to your partner. Your partner writes the sentences.

Writing the Declaration of Independence

The Declaration of Independence said that all men are created equal and have the right to life, liberty, and the pursuit of happiness.

# READ ABOUT IT

**Look and read.**

Signing the Declaration of Independence

The Declaration of Independence was adopted on July 4, 1776. Leaders from the thirteen colonies signed the Declaration of Independence. It said that the colonies were independent from England.

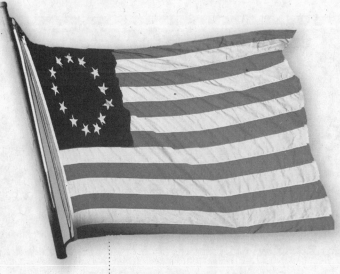

The first U.S. Flag

**Group Work**

Work in groups. Close the book and say the main ideas on this page in your own words.

When the Revolutionary War ended, the thirteen colonies were called states. The new country was called the United States of America. The new flag had thirteen stars and thirteen stripes, one star and one stripe for each state.

# READ ABOUT IT

 **Look and read.**

George Washington

George Washington was in charge of the U.S. Army and Navy during the Revolutionary War. Later he became the first President of the United States. Americans call George Washington the "Father of our Country."

★★★★★★★★★★★★★

**Group Work**

Work in groups. Close the book and say the main ideas on this page in your own words.

George Washington and his First Cabinet by Thomas Pritchard Rossiter

President Washington wanted help making decisions for the new country. He created the Cabinet. The Cabinet is the special group that advises the President.

# WRITE IT DOWN

**Write the sentences.**

1. George Washington was our first President. He created the Cabinet system.

   _____

   _____

2. Thomas Jefferson and other leaders wrote the Declaration of Independence.

   _____

   _____

3. The Declaration of Independence said that all men are created equal.

   _____

   _____

4. The Declaration of Independence also said that all men have the right to life, liberty, and the pursuit of happiness.

   _____

   _____

George Washington

# FIGURE IT OUT

**Complete the dialogs. Use the words from the boxes.**

<table>
<tr><td></td></tr>
<tr><td>George Washington</td></tr>
<tr><td>Father</td></tr>
<tr><td>Revolutionary War</td></tr>
<tr><td>colonies</td></tr>
<tr><td>President</td></tr>
<tr><td>England</td></tr>
<tr><td>Thomas Jefferson</td></tr>
<tr><td>Independence</td></tr>
<tr><td>equal</td></tr>
<tr><td>Declaration</td></tr>
</table>

**A:** In the _____,
Americans fought against England.

**B:** That's right. At that time there were thirteen American

_____.

**A:** _____ was in charge of
the U.S. military.

**B:** He was also our first _____.

**A:** That's why we call him the "_____
of our Country."

**A:** What was the Declaration of _____?

**B:** It said the colonies were independent from _____.

**A:** Who was the main writer of the _____ of
Independence?

**B:** _____. He wrote that all men are created

_____.

**Practice the dialogs with a partner.**

# LESSON 2

## THE CONSTITUTION

**After you finish this lesson, you will be able to talk about**

* ★ the Constitution
* ★ Benjamin Franklin
* ★ the Bill of Rights

### Words to Know
**Practice saying these words.**

| | | |
|---|---|---|
| ★ supreme | ★ speech | ★ citizen |
| ★ amendment | ★ free | ★ vote |
| ★ change | ★ peaceable assembly | ★ benefit |
| ★ rights | ★ peacefully | ★ federal |
| ★ guarantee | ★ petition | ★ passport |

Signing of Constitution

Leaders from the new states wrote the Constitution in 1787 at the Constitutional Convention. The Constitution is the supreme law of the land. It sets up the country's government. There are 27 amendments, or changes, to the Constitution. They guarantee the rights of all people living in the United States.

# TALK IT OVER

**Practice the dialog with a partner.**

**A:** What are the first three words of the Constitution?

**B:** The first three words are "We the People." These words tell about the idea of self-government.

**A:** What's an amendment?

**B:** An amendment is a change to the Constitution.

**A:** How many amendments are there?

**B:** There are 27 amendments, including the Bill of Rights.

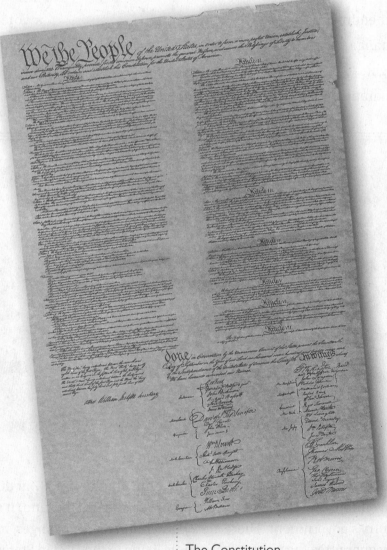

The Constitution

# READ ABOUT IT

**Look and read.**

## The Federalist Papers

After the Constitution was written, the new states had to approve it. Everyone did not support the Constitution. Some thought it gave the national, or federal, government too much power. Three men wrote the Federalist Papers in support of the Constitution. They were James Madison, Alexander Hamilton, and John Jay.

## Benjamin Franklin

Benjamin Franklin was the oldest member of the Constitutional Convention. He was one of the signers of the Declaration of Independence. He was an inventor and a printer. He helped start the first public library and he was the first Postmaster General of the United States. Franklin was also a U.S. diplomat.

# READ ABOUT IT

 **Look and read.**

## The Bill of Rights

The Bill of Rights is the first ten amendments to the Constitution. The Constitution and the Bill of Rights guarantee the rights of all people living in the United States. The government cannot take these rights away.

## Freedom of speech

The First Amendment guarantees freedom of speech. People are free to say what they believe.

**Partner Work**

Take turns. Read the sentences on this page to your partner. Your partner writes the sentences.

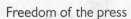

## Signing a petition

The First Amendment guarantees the right to petition, or ask, the government to change.

## Freedom of the press

The First Amendment guarantees freedom of the press. People are free to write and print what they believe.

# READ ABOUT IT

**Look and read.**

Right to assembly

The First Amendment guarantees the right to peaceable assembly. People are free to meet peacefully in groups.

Freedom of religion

The First Amendment guarantees freedom of religion. You can practice any religion you want, or not practice a religion at all.

Fair trial

The Bill of Rights even includes rights for people accused of crimes. In the United States, everyone has the right to a lawyer and a fair trial.

## See for Yourself

If you are interested in reading more about the Bill of Rights, turn to page 82.

# READ ABOUT IT

**Look and read.**

Voting

There are four amendments to the Constitution about who can vote. Citizens eighteen years old and older can vote. Both women and men can vote. A citizen of any race can vote. You do not have to pay a tax to vote.

Susan B. Anthony

Susan B. Anthony fought for women's rights, including the right to vote.

A jury

One responsibility that is only for United States citizens is voting in the country's elections. Another responsibility that is only for United States citizens is serving on a jury.

# READ ABOUT IT

**Look and read.**

This woman is running for office.

Voting is also a right. United States citizens have other rights and benefits. Only U.S. citizens can apply for federal government jobs. Only U.S. citizens can travel with a U.S. passport. Only U.S. citizens can run for office.

Taxes

Most people who earn money in the United States have to pay federal income tax. Those people have to send in tax forms every year. The last day to send in federal income tax forms is April 15.

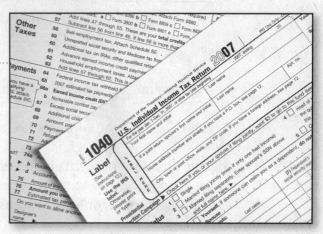

Becoming citizens

When you become a United States citizen, you make promises to the country. You promise to give up loyalty to other countries. You promise to be loyal to the United States. You promise to obey the laws of the United States. You promise to serve, or do important work for, the country.

# FIGURE IT OUT

**Complete the puzzle. Use the words from the box.**

speech
amendment
citizen
Constitution
Franklin
vote
Rights

**Across**

1. Benjamin _____ was the oldest member of the Constitutional Convention.

5. The _____ is the supreme law of the United States.

6. The First Amendment guarantees freedom of _____.

7. One right that is only for citizens is the right to _____.

**Down**

2. A change to the Constitution is called an _____.

3. The first ten amendments to the Constitution is the Bill of _____.

4. A _____ of the United States must be 18 years old to vote.

# LESSON 3

# THE CIVIL WAR

### After you finish this lesson, you will be able to talk about

- ★ the Civil War
- ★ the North and the South
- ★ Abraham Lincoln
- ★ the Emancipation Proclamation

## Words to Know
### Practice saying these words.

| | | |
|---|---|---|
| ★ southern | ★ Union | ★ divide |
| ★ Confederate | ★ slave | ★ unite |
| ★ northern | ★ states' rights | ★ document |

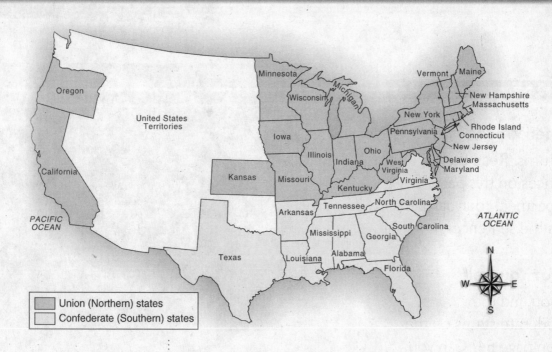

Union (Northern) states
Confederate (Southern) states

The United States in 1863

Americans fought the Civil War from 1861 to 1865. The Southern (Confederate) states wanted to leave the United States and start their own country. They fought against the Northern (Union) states.

# READ ABOUT IT

**Look and read.**

Slaves

The Civil War was fought over slavery and states' rights. Africans were taken to America and sold as slaves. The South wanted to keep slavery. The North wanted to end slavery.

Union soldiers in the Civil War

The North won the Civil War. The Union was saved and slavery ended.

**Partner Work**

Take turns. Read the sentences on this page to your partner. Your partner writes the sentences.

**See for Yourself**

Can you find the Confederate states on the map on page 84? Can you find the Union states?

The Spanish-American War

The United States fought other wars in the 1800s. These were the War of 1812, the Mexican-American War, and the Spanish-American War. After this last war, Puerto Rico and Guam became territories of the United States.

# TALK IT OVER

**Practice the dialogs with a partner.**

**A:** Who was President during the Civil War?

**B:** Abraham Lincoln

**A:** Did the Civil War divide the United States?

**B:** Yes, it did. The states were not united. President Lincoln wanted to keep the country united.


**A:** Abraham Lincoln signed the Emancipation Proclamation.

**B:** What did the Emancipation Proclamation do?

**A:** It freed the slaves.

**B:** That's because Abraham Lincoln wanted freedom for all people.

Abraham Lincoln with
Union soldiers
................

Confederate soldiers
................

# FIGURE IT OUT

**Complete the sentences. Use the words from the box.**

1. The Southern states wanted to keep _____.

2. _____, signed the Emancipation Proclamation.

3. The _____ states were in the South.

4. The _____ freed the slaves.

5. The states in the North were called the _____ states.

> Abraham Lincoln
>
> Confederate
>
> Emancipation
> Proclamation
>
> Union
>
> slavery

**Complete the puzzle. Use the words from the box.**

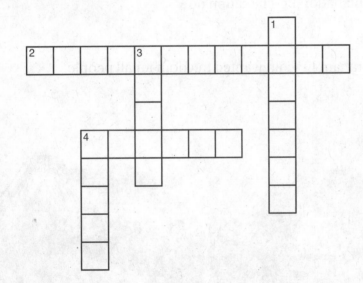

> divided
>
> Union
>
> united
>
> Emancipation
>
> Civil

**Across**

2. The _____ Proclamation said that many slaves were free.

4. The Civil War divided the nation. The states were not _____.

**Down**

1. The Civil War _____ the United States.

3. Abraham Lincoln was President during the _____ War.

4. The North won the war and the _____ was saved.

# LESSON 4

## WORLD WARS I AND II

**After you finish this lesson, you will be able to talk about**

★ World War I
★ the Great Depression
★ World War II
★ the Cold War

### Words to Know
**Practice saying these words.**

★ Europe          ★ ally
★ enter           ★ general
★ enemy           ★ communism

American soldiers during World War I

**See for Yourself**

Where are England, France, and Germany on the map on pages 86–87?

 World War I began in Europe in 1914. The United States entered the war in 1917. Woodrow Wilson was President. The United States, England, France, and Russia fought against Germany and Austria-Hungary.

# TALK IT OVER

**Practice the dialogs with a partner.**

A bread line during the Great Depression

**A:** What happened about ten years after World War I?

**B:** The Great Depression began. It was a hard time.

**A:** Why?

**B:** Many people lost their jobs, money, and homes.

American soldiers during World War II

**A:** The United States entered World War II in 1941. American soldiers fought against Germany, Italy, and Japan.

**B:** Which countries were U.S. allies?

**A:** England, France, and Russia. The Allies won the war in 1945.

# READ ABOUT IT

**Look and read.**

Franklin D. Roosevelt

Franklin D. Roosevelt was elected President during the Great Depression. He was President during most of World War II.

Dwight D. Eisenhower

Dwight D. Eisenhower was a general in World War II. He later became President.

The Berlin Wall

**Group Work**

Work in groups. Close the book and say the main ideas on this page in your own words.

After World War II, a different kind of war began. During the Cold War, the United States was concerned about communism. There was great conflict between the United States and the Soviet Union.

# FIGURE IT OUT

**Match. Next to each numbered item, write the letter of the correct description.**

1. _____
   Woodrow Wilson

2. _____
   The Great Depression

3. _____
   1914

4. _____
   Dwight D. Eisenhower

5. _____
   Germany

6. _____
   1941

7. _____
   Franklin D. Roosevelt

8. _____
   Russia

a.   when World War I began

b.   a country the U.S. fought against in World War I

c.   when the United States entered World War II

d.   a hard time after World War I

e.   the U.S. President during World War II

f.   a U.S. ally in World War II

g.   the U.S. President during World War I

h.   a general during World War II

**Write four complete sentences based on the matching.**

1. _____

_____

2. _____

_____

3. _____

_____

4. _____

_____

# LESSON 5

Track 5

## OTHER MODERN CONFLICTS

**After you finish this lesson, you will be able to talk about**

* ★ the Korean War
* ★ the Vietnam War
* ★ the Persian Gulf War

### Words to Know
**Practice saying these words.**

* ★ Korea
* ★ Communist
* ★ Vietnam
* ★ invade
* ★ assassinate
* ★ protest

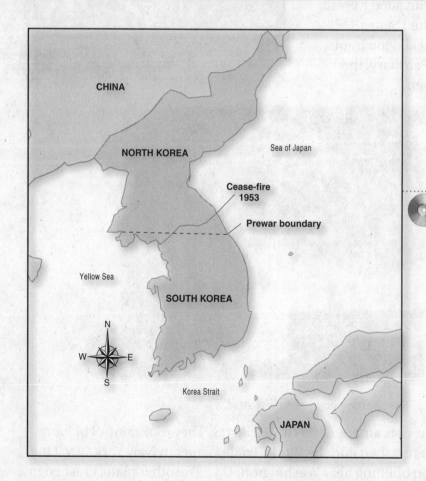

North and South Korea in 1953
.......................................

After World War II, Korea was divided into two parts. North Korea had a communist government. South Korea was a republic. In 1950, North Korea invaded South Korea. The United States and other countries sent soldiers to help South Korea. The Korean War ended in 1953.

# READ ABOUT IT

**Look and read.**

North and South Vietnam in 1954

In 1954 Vietnam was divided into two countries. North Vietnam had a communist government. South Vietnam was a republic. Communists in South Vietnam tried to take over the government. In 1962, the United States sent soldiers to help South Vietnam fight the communists. The Vietnam War lasted until 1973.

Soldiers in the Persian Gulf War

In August 1990, Iraq invaded Kuwait. In January 1991, the United States and other countries attacked the Iraqi invaders. By the end of February, the Persian Gulf War was over.

**Class Discussion**

Ask questions about this page. Other students will answer your questions.

The September 11 terrorist attacks

On September 11, 2001, terrorists attacked the United States. They took control of four American airplanes. Two planes crashed into the World Trade Center in New York City. One plane crashed into the Pentagon building near Washington, D.C. The other plane crashed in a field. Almost 3,000 people were killed. This was the worst terrorist attack in U.S. history.

# FIGURE IT OUT

**Complete the sentences. Use the words from the box.**

| |
|---|
| **Persian Gulf** |
| **terrorists** |
| **1973** |
| **Vietnam** |
| **Korean** |

1. The _____ War ended in 1953.

2. The United States first sent soldiers to _____ in 1962.

3. The Vietnam War ended in _____.

4. The _____ War was fought in 1991.

5. On September 11, 2001, _____ attacked the United States.

American soldiers in Vietnam

# U.S. HISTORY UNIT CHECKUP

**How well did you learn the content in this unit?**
**Fill in the circle in front of the correct answer.**

1. In what year was the Declaration of Independence adopted?
   ○ 1757
   ○ 1775
   ○ 1776
   ○ 1814

2. Which of these is guaranteed by the First Amendment?
   ○ The right to trial by jury in most cases
   ○ The right to bear arms
   ○ Freedom of speech
   ○ The right to happiness

3. What is one reason colonists came to America?
   ○ For religious freedom
   ○ To avoid high taxes
   ○ To fight the British
   ○ To vote

4. Which President freed the slaves?
   ○ Thomas Jefferson
   ○ Abraham Lincoln
   ○ George Washington
   ○ John F. Kennedy

5. What is one reason the colonists fought the British?
   ○ States' rights
   ○ Religious freedom
   ○ Slavery
   ○ Self-government

6. What group of people was taken to America and sold as slaves?
   ○ Native Americans
   ○ Colonists
   ○ Koreans
   ○ Africans

7. Who was the first President of the United States?
   ○ Abraham Lincoln
   ○ George Washington
   ○ Thomas Jefferson
   ○ Patrick Henry

8. Whose rights are guaranteed by the Constitution and the Bill of Rights?
   ○ All people living in the United States
   ○ Registered voters
   ○ The President
   ○ Natural born citizens

9. What is a change to the Constitution called?
   ○ An amendment
   ○ Congress
   ○ A right
   ○ The Preamble

10. What was the main concern of the United States during the Cold War?
   ○ Terrorism
   ○ Civil rights
   ○ Communism
   ○ States' rights

11. What are the 13 original states?
    - ○ Virginia, Massachusetts, Maryland, Rhode Island, Connecticut, New Hampshire, North Carolina, South Carolina, New York, New Zealand, Pennsylvania, Delaware, Georgia
    - ○ Virginia, Massachusetts, Maryland, Rhode Island, Connecticut, New Hampshire, North Carolina, South Carolina, New York, New Jersey, Pennsylvania, Delaware, Georgia
    - ○ Virginia, Massachusetts, Maryland, Rhode Island, Connecticut, Kentucky, North Carolina, South Carolina, New York, New Jersey, Pennsylvania, Delaware, Georgia
    - ○ Virginia, Massachusetts, Maryland, Washington, D.C., Connecticut, New Hampshire, North Carolina, South Carolina, New York, New Jersey, Pennsylvania, Delaware, Georgia

12. Who was the President during the Civil War?
    - ○ George Washington
    - ○ Ulysses S. Grant
    - ○ Abraham Lincoln
    - ○ Thomas Jefferson

13. What is one responsibility that is only for U.S. citizens?
    - ○ Paying income taxes
    - ○ Voting
    - ○ Registering for the Selective Service
    - ○ Pursuing happiness

14. "We the people" are the first three words of what document?
    - ○ The Emancipation Proclamation
    - ○ The Constitution
    - ○ The Bill of Rights
    - ○ The Declaration of Independence

15. What was one problem that led to the Civil War?
    - ○ High taxes
    - ○ States' rights
    - ○ Communism
    - ○ Women's rights

16. What is one war fought by the United States in the 1900s?
    - ○ The Civil War
    - ○ The Revolutionary War
    - ○ World War I
    - ○ The Mexican-American War

17. What is one right in the Declaration of Independence?
    - ○ Freedom of speech
    - ○ Liberty
    - ○ Voting
    - ○ Running for office

18. Where does freedom of speech come from?
    - ○ The Declaration of Independence
    - ○ The President
    - ○ The Emancipation Proclamation
    - ○ The Bill of Rights

**19.** How many amendments are there to the Constitution?
- ○ 9
- ○ 10
- ○ 13
- ○ 27

**20.** From whom did the United States gain independence in the Revolutionary War?
- ○ France
- ○ Germany
- ○ Japan
- ○ England

**21.** When did terrorists attack the United States?
- ○ September 11, 2001
- ○ April 15, 2005
- ○ July 4, 1999
- ○ January 1, 2004

**22.** Who is called the "Father of our Country"?
- ○ Thomas Jefferson
- ○ John Adams
- ○ George Washington
- ○ Abraham Lincoln

**23.** What are the first ten amendments to the Constitution called?
- ○ The Preamble
- ○ The Bill of Rights
- ○ The First Ten Amendments
- ○ The Declaration of Independence

**24.** In what year was the Constitution written?
- ○ 1876
- ○ 1776
- ○ 1814
- ○ 1787

**25.** What special group advises the President?
- ○ Congress
- ○ The army
- ○ The Cabinet
- ○ The Constitution

**26.** A United States citizen has to be at least what age to vote?
- ○ 16
- ○ 18
- ○ 35
- ○ 21

**27.** What did the Emancipation Proclamation do?
- ○ It freed the Native Americans (American Indians).
- ○ It ended the Civil War.
- ○ It freed the slaves.
- ○ It ended World War II.

**28.** What is one promise you make when you become a United States citizen?
- ○ To be loyal to the United States
- ○ To run for office
- ○ To carry a U.S. passport
- ○ To vote

**29.** When is the last day to send in federal income tax forms?
- ○ April 15
- ○ July 4
- ○ September 11
- ○ December 25

**30.** Who was the main writer of the Declaration of Independence?
- ○ George Washington
- ○ Abraham Lincoln
- ○ Patrick Henry
- ○ Thomas Jefferson

**31.** What is the supreme law of the United States?
- ○ The Preamble
- ○ The Bill of Rights
- ○ The Emancipation Proclamation
- ○ The Constitution

**32.** Who did the United States fight in World War II?
- ○ Germany, Italy, and Japan
- ○ England, France, and Russia
- ○ North Vietnam and South Vietnam
- ○ Germany and Austria-Hungary

# TALK ABOUT IT

**Talk about what you learned in this unit. Work with a partner. What would you like to learn more about? Make a list.**

_____

_____

_____

_____

_____

_____

_____

**Share one idea with the class.**

# UNIT 2

## U.S. GOVERNMENT

### *What do you know about the government of the United States of America?*

☆ **What are the three branches of the U.S. government?**

☆ **What branch makes the laws?**

☆ **What are the two major political parties?**

---

**1789**
Congress meets
for the first time

**1800**
John Adams is the first President
to move into the White House

**1791**
The Bill of Rights becomes
part of the Constitution

**1860**
Abraham Lincoln becomes
President

**1945**
The United Nations
is created

**1981**
Sandra Day O' Connor is
the first woman Supreme
Court justice

**1959**
Alaska and Hawaii become
the 49th and 50th states

## THE LEGISLATIVE BRANCH

**After you finish this lesson, you will be able to talk about**

* ★ the legislative branch
* ★ Congress
* ★ the House of Representatives
* ★ the Senate

### Words to Know
**Practice saying these words.**

| | | |
|---|---|---|
| ★ branch | ★ elect | ★ serve |
| ★ legislative | ★ senator | ★ Vice President |
| ★ executive | ★ representative | ★ Speaker of the House |
| ★ judicial | ★ federal | |

Congress makes
the laws.

The Constitution set up the U.S. government in three branches—the legislative, the executive, and the judicial. This separation of powers stops any one branch of government from becoming too powerful. The legislative branch makes laws. Another name for the legislative branch is Congress.

# READ ABOUT IT

**Look and read.**

A representative at work in her office

Senators work in the Senate. There are 100 U.S. senators. Representatives work in the House of Representatives. There are 435 voting members in the House of Representatives.

Nancy Pelosi is the Speaker of the House of Representatives.

The two parts of the U.S. Congress are the Senate and the House of Representatives.

The U.S. entered World War II after Congress declared war in 1941.

Congress makes the federal laws of the United States.

The U.S. Capitol building

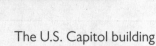

Congress meets in the Capitol building. This building is in Washington, D.C., the capital of the United States.

## Partner Work

Take turns. Read the sentences on this page to your partner. Your partner writes the sentences.

## See for Yourself

Can you find Washington, D.C., on the map on pages 84–85?

# WRITE IT DOWN

**Write the sentences.**

1. There are 100 senators in Congress. Senators represent all the people of a state.

   _____

   _____

2. There are 435 voting members in the House of Representatives.

   _____

   _____

3. We elect a U.S. senator for six years. We elect a U.S. representative for two years.

   _____

   _____

4. Some states have more representatives than other states because they have more people.

   _____

   _____

5. The Vice President is the leader of the Senate. The Speaker of the House is the leader of the House of Representatives.

   _____

   _____

   _____

   _____

# FIGURE IT OUT

**Complete the chart. Use the numbers from the box.**

| |
|:---:|
| 6 |
| 100 |
| 2 |
| 435 |

## Congress

### The House of Representatives

1. _____ representatives

2. Elected every _____ years

States that have more people have more representatives in the House.

Must be a citizen—either born in the United States or naturalized

### The Senate

1. _____ senators

2. Elected every _____ years

Each state has two senators.

Must be a citizen—either born in the United States or naturalized

Inside the U.S. Capitol building

Congress meets in the Capitol building. This building is in Washington, D.C., the capital of the United States.

# LESSON 7

## THE EXECUTIVE BRANCH

**After you finish this lesson, you will be able to talk about**

★ the executive branch
★ the President
★ the Vice President

**Words to Know**
**Practice saying these words.**

★ enforce          ★ sign bills into law          ★ term
★ official         ★ veto                         ★ requirement

President George W. Bush
in his office in the White House

The President, the Cabinet, and departments under the Cabinet members are the executive branch of the U.S. government. The President is in charge of the executive branch. The executive branch enforces the law.

# READ ABOUT IT

**Look and read.**

President Obama and Vice Président Biden were elected together.

The Vice President is elected with the President.

President Bush and his Cabinet

The Cabinet advises the President. Some Cabinet-level positions are the Attorney General and the Secretaries of Defense, Education, Energy, Homeland Security, State, Labor, and the Treasury.

President Johnson signing the Civil Rights Act of 1964

The President signs bills to make them laws and also vetoes bills. The President is Commander in Chief of the U.S. military.

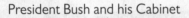

★★★★★★★★★★★★★★★★

**Group Work**

Work in groups. Close the book and say the main ideas on this page in your own words.

Vice President Lyndon Johnson became President when John Kennedy was assassinated.

If the President is unable to serve, the Vice President becomes President. If both the President and the Vice President are unable to serve, the Speaker of the House becomes President.

# TALK IT OVER

**Practice the dialogs with a partner.**

**A:**    For how many years is the President elected?

**B:**    Four years

**A:**    When do we vote for the President?

**B:**    November

**A:**    How old do citizens have to be to vote for President?

**B:**    Eighteen and older

The 1932 election

**A:**    What is the name of the President of the United States now?

**B:**    Barack Obama

**A:**    What is the name of the Vice President of the United States now?

**B:**    Joe Biden

**A:**    What is the political party of the President now?

**B:**    Democratic

# FIGURE IT OUT

**Complete the chart. Make a ✓ in the correct column.**

|  | **The President** | **The Vice President** |
|---|---|---|
| **1.** becomes President if the President can no longer serve |  |  |
| **2.** is the Commander in Chief of the U.S. military |  |  |
| **3.** is in charge of the executive branch of the government |  |  |
| **4.** is elected with the President |  |  |
| **5.** vetoes bills |  |  |

**Complete the sentences. Use the words and numbers from the box to answer 1–5.**

1. The President is elected for _____ years.

2. The political party of the President now is _____.

3. The President is elected in _____.

4. The name of the President of the United States

   now is _____.

5. The name of the Vice President of the United States

   now is _____.

| Barack Obama |
| November |
| 4 |
| Democratic |
| Joe Biden |

# LESSON 8

## THE JUDICIAL BRANCH

**After you finish this lesson, you will be able to talk about**

★ the judicial branch
★ the Supreme Court

### Words to Know
**Practice saying these words.**

| | | |
|---|---|---|
| ★ justice | ★ agree | ★ nominate |
| ★ review | ★ decision | ★ approve |
| ★ resolve | ★ final | |
| ★ dispute | ★ choose | |

Visitors waiting outside the
Supreme Court Building

The Supreme Court is the highest part of the judicial branch of the U.S. government. The nine Supreme Court justices review and explain the law. They make sure that the laws agree with the Constitution. They also resolve disputes. The Chief Justice is in charge of the Supreme Court.

# Talk It Over

**Practice the dialogs with a partner.**

**A:** The Supreme Court is the highest court in the United States, right?

**B:** Yes, the decisions of the Supreme Court justices are final.

**A:** What is the "rule of law"?

**B:** Everyone must follow the law, including leaders and the government.

The nine justices of the Supreme Court

**A:** How many justices are on the Supreme Court?

**B:** Nine, including the Chief Justice

**A:** Who is the Chief Justice now?

**B:** John Roberts

Chief Justice John Roberts

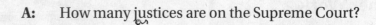

# WRITE IT DOWN

**Write the sentences.**

1. The three branches of the U.S. government are the legislative, executive, and judicial branches.

   _____

   _____

2. The Supreme Court is the highest part of the judicial branch. It is the highest court in the United States.

   _____

   _____

3. The judicial branch decides if laws agree with the Constitution. It reviews laws, explains laws, and resolves disputes.

   _____

   _____

4. There are nine Supreme Court justices. John Roberts is the Chief Justice of the United States.

   _____

   _____

**Partner Work**

Take turns. Read the sentences on this page to your partner. Your partner writes the sentences.

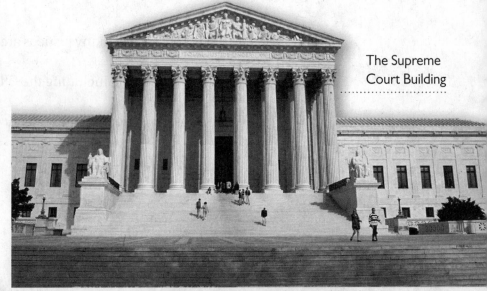

The Supreme Court Building

# FIGURE IT OUT

**Complete the sentences. Use the words from the box.**

1. The _____ decides if the

   laws agree with the Constitution.

2. _____ is the Chief Justice

   of the United States.

3. _____ approves the

   Supreme Court justices.

> **Congress**
>
> **Supreme Court**
>
> **John Roberts**

**Complete the chart. Write the branch of government. Use the words from the box.**

| The Three Branches of U.S. Government |
| --- |
| 1. _____ <br> • enforces the laws <br> • The President is in charge. |
| 2. _____ <br> • makes the laws <br> • the Senate and the House of Representatives |
| 3. _____ <br> • interprets the law <br> • has nine justices |

> **Judicial**
>
> **Legislative**
>
> **Executive**

## STATES AND CAPITALS

**After you finish this lesson, you will be able to talk about**

★ the U.S. government

★ federal and state levels of government

★ capital cities

 **Words to Know**
**Practice saying these words.**

★ own
  am

★ make laws

★ capital

★ legislature

★ governor

The New York state legislature meets in this building in Albany, New York.

 There are fifty states in the United States. Each state has its own government. Each state government can make its own laws. But these laws must agree with the U.S. Constitution. Most state governments have three branches—legislative, executive, and judicial.

# READ ABOUT IT

**Look and read.**

Governors meet

Every state has a governor. The governor is in charge of the executive branch of the state government. All the state governors meet with each other once a year.

**Complete the sentences. Write about the state you live in.**

1. The name of the state I live in is _____.

2. The capital of my state is _____.

3. The two senators from my state are _____

    and _____.

4. The governor of my state is _____.

5. The name of my U.S. representative is

    _____.

**See for Yourself**

Can you find your state on the map on pages 84–85?

# READ ABOUT IT

 **Look and read. Then circle your state and state capital.**

The government of each state is in the state capital.

## Map Key

| State | State Capital |
|---|---|
| Alabama | ★Montgomery |
| Alaska | ★Juneau |
| Arizona | ★Phoenix |
| Arkansas | ★Little Rock |
| California | ★Sacramento |
| Colorado | ★Denver |
| Connecticut | ★Hartford |
| Delaware | ★Dover |
| Florida | ★Tallahassee |
| Georgia | ★Atlanta |
| Hawaii | ★Honolulu |
| Idaho | ★Boise |
| Illinois | ★Springfield |
| Indiana | ★Indianapolis |
| Iowa | ★Des Moines |

| | |
|---|---|
| Kansas | ★Topeka |
| Kentucky | ★Frankfort |
| Louisiana | ★Baton Rouge |
| Maine | ★Augusta |
| Maryland | ★Annapolis |
| Massachusetts | ★Boston |
| Michigan | ★Lansing |
| Minnesota | ★St. Paul |
| Mississippi | ★Jackson |
| Missouri | ★Jefferson City |
| Montana | ★Helena |
| Nebraska | ★Lincoln |
| Nevada | ★Carson City |
| New Hampshire | ★Concord |
| New Jersey | ★Trenton |
| New Mexico | ★Santa Fe |
| New York | ★Albany |
| North Carolina | ★Raleigh |

| | |
|---|---|
| North Dakota | ★Bismarck |
| Ohio | ★Columbus |
| Oklahoma | ★Oklahoma City |
| Oregon | ★Salem |
| Pennsylvania | ★Harrisburg |
| Rhode Island | ★Providence |
| South Carolina | ★Columbia |
| South Dakota | ★Pierre |
| Tennessee | ★Nashville |
| Texas | ★Austin |
| Utah | ★Salt Lake City |
| Vermont | ★Montpelier |
| Virginia | ★Richmond |
| Washington | ★Olympia |
| West Virginia | ★Charleston |
| Wisconsin | ★Madison |
| Wyoming | ★Cheyenne |

# FIGURE IT OUT

**Plan a trip. Below is the map of your trip. Look at the map on page 50 to find the names of the cities and states you will be visiting. Write the names on the lines below.**

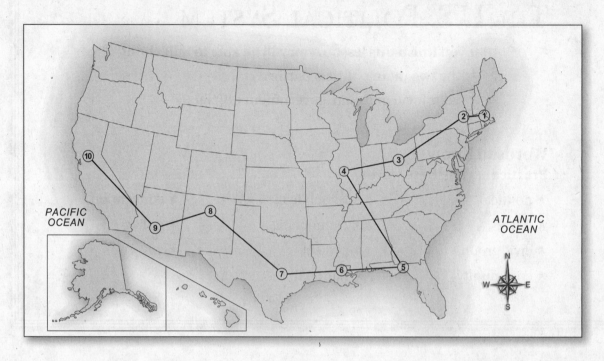

|  | **Capital** | **State** |
|---|---|---|
| 1. | _____ | _____ |
| 2. | _____ | _____ |
| 3. | _____ | _____ |
| 4. | _____ | _____ |
| 5. | _____ | _____ |
| 6. | _____ | _____ |
| 7. | _____ | _____ |
| 8. | _____ | _____ |
| 9. | _____ | _____ |
| 10. | _____ | _____ |

# LESSON 10

Track 10

# THE U.S. POLITICAL SYSTEM

**After you finish this lesson, you will be able to talk about**

★ the two main political parties

★ your local and state government officials

## Words to Know
**Practice saying these words.**

| | | |
|---|---|---|
| ★ political | ★ Republican | ★ convention |
| ★ party | ★ Democratic | ★ policy |
| ★ civic group | ★ protect | ★ governor |
| ★ community | ★ national | |

Americans vote for their leaders.

Americans can participate in their democracy by voting. They can join a political party, civic group, or community group. They can help with a campaign, run for office, call senators and representatives, or write to a newspaper.

# READ ABOUT IT

**Look and read.**

The Republican and Democratic candidates for President in 2008

There are two major political parties in the United States. They are the Republican and the Democratic parties. The parties want to work for and protect the country. They both work on the national, state, and local levels.

The Democratic National Convention in 2008

Every four years the Democrats and Republicans have large meetings called conventions. The parties decide on their leaders and policies at these conventions.

**Class Discussion**

Ask questions about this page. Other students will answer your questions.

# WRITE IT DOWN

Complete the charts. Federal, state, and city governments have three branches.
Use the names of the people who hold these offices today.

| FEDERAL | | |
|---|---|---|
| **Executive Branch** | **Legislative Branch** | **Judicial Branch** |
| President:<br><br>_____<br><br>Vice President:<br><br>_____<br><br>Party:<br><br>_____ | Senators:<br><br>_____<br><br>_____<br><br>Representative(s):<br><br>_____<br><br>_____ | Chief Justice:<br><br>_____ |

| STATE _____ (your state) | | |
|---|---|---|
| **Executive Branch** | **Legislative Branch** | **Judicial Branch** |
| Governor:<br><br>_____<br><br>Party:<br><br>_____ | State Senators:<br><br>_____<br><br>_____<br><br>Representative:<br><br>_____ | Chief Justice:<br><br>_____ |

# WRITE IT DOWN

**Read the chart. Then write which powers belong to state government and which belong to the federal government.**

|  | State Government | Federal Government |
|---|:---:|:---:|
| **1.** Print money | | |
| **2.** Provide protection and safety | | |
| **3.** Declare war | | |
| **4.** Give a driver's license | | |
| **5.** Create an army | | |
| **6.** Make treaties | | |
| **7.** Provide education | ✓ | |

**Complete the sentences.**

1. Branches of state government are

   _____

   _____

2. Branches of the federal government are

   _____

   _____

**Write the sentences.**

1. The Democratic and Republican parties are the two major political parties in the United States.

   _____

   _____

2. The President is elected for a term of four years.

   _____

   _____

# READ ABOUT IT

 **Look and read.**

The New York Stock Exchange building on Wall Street

The economic system in the United States is a capitalist, or free market, economy. Businesses compete freely with each other. The government does not control the supply or the price of goods and services.

# FIGURE IT OUT

**Complete the chart. Where can you find this person? Make a ✓.**

|  | Federal Government | State Government |
|---|---|---|
| 1. Governor |  |  |
| 2. State senator |  |  |
| 3. President |  |  |
| 4. Chief Justice |  |  |
| 5. U.S. Senator |  |  |

**Complete the sentences. Circle the answer. Then write the sentence.**

1. The form of government in the United States is a (democracy, dictatorship).

   _____

   _____

2. There are (two, three) major political parties in the United States.

   _____

   _____

3. One is the Democratic party. One is the (Republican, Executive) party.

   _____

   _____

4. The three (parties, branches) of the U.S. government are the legislative, the executive, and the judicial.

   _____

   _____

# U.S. HISTORY UNIT CHECKUP

**How well did you learn the content in this unit?**
**Fill in the circle in front of the correct answer.**

1. Who is the Chief Justice of the United
   States?
   ○ George W. Bush
   ○ John Roberts
   ○ Thomas Jefferson
   ○ Dick Cheney

2. What is the highest court in the United
   States?
   ○ The Constitution
   ○ The President
   ○ Congress
   ○ The Supreme Court

3. What are the three branches of our
   government?
   ○ Democratic, Republican, Independent
   ○ Department of Justice, Department of
      State, Department of Defense
   ○ Executive, Judicial, Legislative
   ○ Police, Education, Legislative

4. What is the "rule of law"?
   ○ The police are in charge.
   ○ Everyone must follow the law.
   ○ Leaders are above the law.
   ○ The President makes the law.

5. What is one power of the states?
   ○ Provide schooling and education
   ○ Print money
   ○ Make treaties
   ○ Declare war

6. Why do some states have more
   representatives than other states?
   ○ Because of the number of people in the
      state
   ○ Because of the size of land covered by
      the state
   ○ Because of the state's economy
   ○ Because of the state's history

7. Which of the following is a Cabinet-level
   position?
   ○ Secretary of State
   ○ Senator
   ○ Representative
   ○ Governor

8. In what month do we vote for the
   President?
   ○ January
   ○ July
   ○ June
   ○ November

9. What stops one branch of government from
   becoming too powerful?
   ○ Unification of powers
   ○ The executive branch
   ○ Congress
   ○ Separation of powers

10. Who is in charge of the executive branch?
   ○ The President
   ○ Congress
   ○ The Supreme Court
   ○ The Vice President

11. Who does a U.S. senator represent?
    ○ The people in one area of a state
    ○ All people of a state
    ○ The governor of a state
    ○ The President

12. What does the President's Cabinet do?
    ○ Makes laws
    ○ Advises the President
    ○ In charge of the executive branch
    ○ Advises the Supreme Court

13. Who becomes President if the President and the Vice President can no longer serve?
    ○ The Speaker of the House of Representatives
    ○ The Senate Majority Leader
    ○ The Chairman of the Joint Chiefs of Staff
    ○ The Chief Justice of the Supreme Court

14. Who is the Commander in Chief of the U.S. military?
    ○ The President
    ○ The Chief Justice of the Supreme Court
    ○ The Vice President
    ○ The Speaker of the House of Representatives

15. What is the legislative branch of our government?
    ○ Congress
    ○ The Supreme Court
    ○ The presidency
    ○ The House of Representatives

16. How many justices are there on the Supreme Court?
    ○ 3
    ○ 9
    ○ 10
    ○ 13

17. What is the name of the President of the United States now?
    ○ Barack Obama
    ○ George W. Bush
    ○ Dick Cheney
    ○ Joe Biden

18. What does the judicial branch do?
    ○ Creates laws
    ○ Enforces laws
    ○ Vetoes laws
    ○ Reviews laws

19. What is the executive branch of our government?
    ○ The President, the Cabinet, and the departments under the Cabinet
    ○ The states
    ○ The House of Representatives and the Senate
    ○ The Supreme Court

20. What are the two major political parties in the United States?
    ○ The House of Representatives and the Senate
    ○ The President and the Vice President
    ○ Democratic and Republican
    ○ Congress and the Supreme Court

**21.** Which of the following is not a power of the federal government?
- ○ To print money
- ○ To give a driver's license
- ○ To declare war
- ○ To make treaties

**22.** Who signs bills to make them laws?
- ○ The Supreme Court
- ○ Congress
- ○ The President
- ○ The Senate

**23.** How many U.S. senators are there?
- ○ 50
- ○ 100
- ○ 102
- ○ 435

**24.** What are the two parts of the U.S. Congress?
- ○ Democrats and Republicans
- ○ The Senate and the House of Representatives
- ○ The executive branch of government
- ○ The judicial branch of government

**25.** Who makes federal laws in the United States?
- ○ The President
- ○ The Speaker of the House
- ○ The Chief Justice of the Supreme Court
- ○ Congress

**26.** What is the political party of the President now?
- ○ Republican
- ○ Democratic
- ○ Independent
- ○ Green

**27.** The House of Representatives has how many voting members?
- ○ 52
- ○ 100
- ○ 435
- ○ 500

**28.** Name one branch of the United States government.
- ○ Democrat
- ○ Republican
- ○ Independent
- ○ Judicial

**29.** We elect a President for how many years?
- ○ 2 years
- ○ There is no limit.
- ○ 4 years
- ○ 6 years

**30.** If the President can no longer serve, who becomes President?
- ○ One of the senators
- ○ The Chief Justice
- ○ The leader of the Cabinet
- ○ The Vice President

**31.** What is the economic system in the United States?
- ○ Command economy
- ○ Market economy
- ○ Socialist economy
- ○ Federal reserve

**32.** Where is the capital of the United States?
- ○ Washington, D.C.
- ○ New York, NY
- ○ Atlanta, GA
- ○ Boston, MA

# TALK ABOUT IT

**Talk about what you learned in this unit. Work with a partner.**
**What would you like to learn more about? Make a list.**

_____

_____

_____

_____

_____

_____

_____

_____

_____

**Share one idea with the class.**

# UNIT 3

## INTEGRATED CIVICS

### What do you know about geography, holidays, and symbols in the United States of America?

☆ **What was the first American holiday?**

☆ **Why is July 4 an important day for Americans?**

☆ **What is the "Star-Spangled Banner?**

| January<br>Martin Luther King, Jr. Day | | May<br>Memorial Day | July<br>Independence Day |
|---|---|---|---|
| | February<br>Presidents' Day | | |

November
Veterans Day

September
Labor Day

November
Thanksgiving

# LESSON 11

## GEOGRAPHY

**After you finish this lesson, you will be able to talk about**

★ **United States geography**
★ **States that border Canada and Mexico**
★ **The U.S. Territories**

### Words to Know
**Practice saying these words.**

★ Atlantic        ★ west        ★ river
★ Pacific         ★ border      ★ territory
★ east            ★ ocean       ★ tribe

The Pacific Ocean

The Atlantic Ocean

 The Pacific Ocean is on the West Coast of the United States. The Atlantic Ocean is on the East Coast of the United States.

# READ ABOUT IT

**Look at the map and read.**

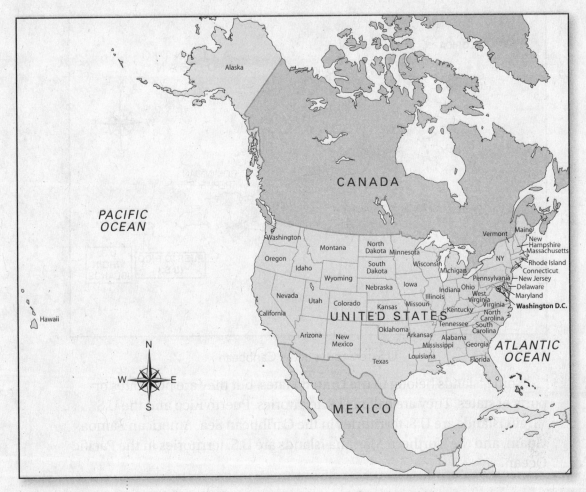

Map of United States and land areas of Canada and Mexico

Thirteen states border, or are next to, Canada. They are Maine, New Hampshire, Vermont, New York, Pennsylvania, Ohio, Michigan, Minnesota, North Dakota, Montana, Idaho, Washington, and Alaska.

Four states border, or are next to, Mexico. They are California, Arizona, New Mexico, and Texas.

The two longest rivers in the United States are the Mississippi River and the Missouri River. In 1803, the United States bought a large area of land near these rivers from France. This land was called the Louisiana Territory. Part of this land is now the state of Louisiana.

The capital of the United States is Washington, D.C.

# READ ABOUT IT

**Look at the map and read.**

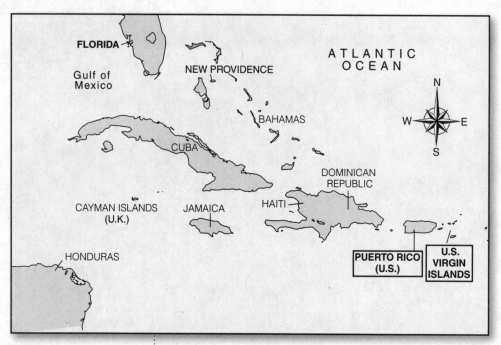

U.S. territories in the Caribbean

Some islands belong to the United States, but they are not states or parts of states. They are called U.S. territories. Puerto Rico and the U.S. Virgin Islands are U.S. territories in the Caribbean Sea. American Samoa, Guam, and the Northern Mariana Islands are U.S. territories in the Pacific Ocean.

Native American today celebrating traditions from the past

Before the Europeans arrived in America, Native Americans lived here. Native Americans are also called American Indians. There were hundreds of tribes, or groups, of Native Americans across North America. Many tribes still exist. Some tribes are Cherokee, Sioux, Crow, Navajo, and Hopi.

# FIGURE IT OUT

**Complete the sentences. Use the words from the box.
You can look at the maps in this lesson for help.**

| |
|---|
| **Cherokee** |
| **Mississippi** |
| **West Coast** |
| **New York** |
| **Hopi** |
| **Idaho** |
| **Arizona** |
| **New Mexico** |
| **Atlantic** |
| **Louisiana** |
| **Guam** |

1. The Pacific Ocean is on the _____ of the United States.

2. Two states that border Canada are _____ and _____ .

3. The _____ Ocean is on the East Coast of the United States.

4. The United States bought the _____ Territory from France in 1803.

5. _____ is a U.S. territory.

6. Two American Indian tribes in the United States are _____ and _____ .

7. Two states that border Mexico are _____ and _____ .

8. One of the two longest rivers in the United States is the _____ River.

The Mississippi River

**Track 12**

# LESSON 12

## THANKSGIVING

**After you finish this lesson, you will be able to talk about**

- ★ the Pilgrims and Native Americans
- ★ Thanksgiving

### Words to Know
**Practice saying these words.**

| | | |
|---|---|---|
| ★ holiday | ★ religious freedom | ★ hunt |
| ★ celebrate | ★ the *Mayflower* | ★ fish |
| ★ sail | ★ plant | ★ harvest |
| ★ gain | ★ corn | ★ meal |

A Thanksgiving celebration

 Thanksgiving was the first American holiday. Americans celebrate Thanksgiving on the fourth Thursday in November. On Thanksgiving Day, Americans give thanks for the good things in their lives. They share a special meal with their family and friends.

# READ ABOUT IT

**Look and read.**

The *Mayflower*

In 1620 a group of people sailed from England to gain religious freedom. The people were Pilgrims. Their ship was the *Mayflower*.

★★★★★★★★★★★★★★

**Group Work**
Work in groups. Close the book and say the main ideas on this page in your own words.

Winter was hard for the Pilgrims.

The first winter in America was hard for the Pilgrims. They had little food. Native Americans helped the Pilgrims plant corn and hunt and fish. To celebrate the first harvest, the Pilgrims and the Native Americans shared a large meal.

# FIGURE IT OUT

Complete the puzzle. Use the words from the box.

Mayflower
meal
Native Americans
Pilgrims
November
freedom

**Across**

2. _____ helped the Pilgrims.

4. The _____ left England in 1620.

5. The Pilgrims left England to find religious _____.

**Down**

1. After the harvest, they had a large _____.

2. Americans celebrate Thanksgiving in _____.

3. The Pilgrims came to America on the _____.

The first Thanksgiving

# LESSON 13

# INDEPENDENCE DAY AND NATIONAL SYMBOLS

**After you finish this lesson you will be able to talk about**

* ★ Independence Day
* ★ The "Star-Spangled Banner"
* ★ the U.S. flag

## Words to Know
**Practice saying these words.**

* ★ picnic
* ★ parade
* ★ fly the flag

* ★ song
* ★ national anthem
* ★ star

* ★ stripe
* ★ banner

An Independence Day parade

 We celebrate Independence Day on the Fourth of July. On this day, Americans remember the signing of the Declaration of Independence on July 4, 1776. People have picnics and parades and fly the flag.

# TALK IT OVER

**Practice the dialog with a partner.**

A Fourth of July celebration in Washington, D.C.

**A:**   When do we celebrate Independence Day?

**B:**   July 4

**A:**   Why is Independence Day important?

**B:**   On July 4, 1776, leaders of the thirteen colonies signed the Declaration of Independence and the colonies became independent from England.

# READ ABOUT IT

**Look and read.**

The Statue of Liberty

**The Statue of Liberty**

The Statue of Liberty stands on Liberty Island in New York Harbor.

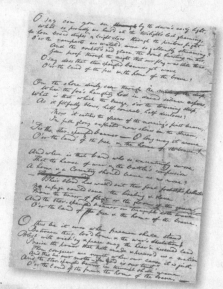

**The "Star-Spangled Banner"**

The "Star-Spangled Banner" is the national anthem of the United States.

**Saying the Pledge of Allegiance**

We show loyalty to the United States and the flag when we say the Pledge of Allegiance.

## Class Discussion

Ask questions about this page. Other students will answer your questions.

## See for Yourself

If you are interested in learning more about the "Star-Spangled Banner," turn to page 83.

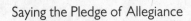

**The U.S. flag today**

The U.S. flag has fifty stars. There is a star for each state. The flag has thirteen stripes. There is one stripe for each of the thirteen original colonies.

# WRITE IT DOWN

**Write the sentences.**

The U.S. flag in 1777

1. The United States began with thirteen colonies.

   _____

   _____

2. The flag has thirteen stripes, one stripe for each of the thirteen original colonies.

   _____

   _____

**Partner Work**

Take turns. Read the sentences on this page to your partner. Your partner writes the sentences.

3. Now the United States has fifty states.

   _____

   _____

4. The flag has fifty stars, one star for each state.

   _____

   _____

# FIGURE IT OUT

**Complete the puzzle. Use the words from the box.**

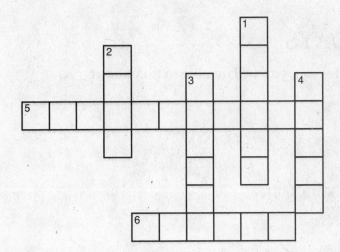

July
parade
Union
stripe
Banner
Declaration

**Across**

5. Americans remember the signing of the _____ of Independence on the Fourth of July.

6. Many cities celebrate Independence Day with a _____ .

**Down**

1. There is a _____ on the flag for each of the thirteen colonies.

2. _____ 4 is America's birthday.

3. The "Star-Spangled _____ " is the name of the national anthem.

4. There is a star on the flag for every state in the _____ .

**Complete the sentences. Use the words from the puzzle.**

1. There are thirteen _____s on the flag.

2. Today there are fifty states in the _____ .

3. _____ is another word for flag.

4. Independence Day is in _____ .

5. Americans celebrate the Fourth of July with picnics and _____s.

6. Thomas Jefferson wrote the _____ of Independence.

# LESSON 14

Track 14

## OTHER HOLIDAYS

**After you finish this lesson, you will be able to talk about**

* ★ President's Day
* ★ Veteran's Day
* ★ Labor Day
* ★ Memorial Day
* ★ Martin Luther King, Jr. Day

### Words to Know
**Practice saying these words.**

| | | |
|---|---|---|
| ★ get time off | ★ worker | ★ civil rights |
| ★ honor | ★ discrimination | ★ win |

Americans enjoy celebrating holidays with their families.

American holidays honor special people or times in U.S. history. Banks and schools often close. Many people get time off from work and school.

# Read About It

**Look and read.**

George Washington and Abraham Lincoln

President's Day honors two great Presidents—George Washington and Abraham Lincoln. President's Day is the third Monday in February.

A Labor Day parade honoring American workers

Labor Day honors American workers. Labor Day is the first Monday in September.

The Vietnam War Memorial honors the Americans who died in that war.

On Memorial Day, we remember the men and women who died in war. Memorial Day is the last Monday in May.

Veteran's Day ceremony

On Veteran's Day, Americans remember the men and women who served in the United States armed forces. Veteran's Day is November 11.

## Partner Work

Take turns. Read the sentences on this page to your partner. Your partner writes the sentences.

# READ ABOUT IT

**Look and read.**

A civil rights march

In parts of the United States, there were laws that separated white people and black people. In the 1950s and 1960s, the civil rights movement tried to end racial discrimination. People in the movement worked for equality for all Americans.

Dr. Martin Luther King, Jr. in his office in 1966

Dr. Martin Luther King, Jr. was a civil rights leader. He fought for civil rights. He helped black Americans win the rights guaranteed to them in the Constitution. Dr. King worked hard to change laws that were not fair. His birthday is a national holiday and is celebrated on the third Monday in January.

# FIGURE IT OUT

**Circle the dates of these holidays for this sample calendar.**

Veteran's Day

Memorial Day

Independence Day

Martin Luther King, Jr. Day

Labor Day

President's Day

**January**

| Sun | Mon | Tue | Wed | Thu | Fri | Sat |
|-----|-----|-----|-----|-----|-----|-----|
|     |     | 1   | 2   | 3   | 4   | 5   |
| 6   | 7   | 8   | 9   | 10  | 11  | 12  |
| 13  | 14  | 15  | 16  | 17  | 18  | 19  |
| 20  | 21  | 22  | 23  | 24  | 25  | 26  |
| 27  | 28  | 29  | 30  | 31  |     |     |

**February**

| Sun | Mon | Tue | Wed | Thu | Fri | Sat |
|-----|-----|-----|-----|-----|-----|-----|
| 3   | 4   | 5   | 6   | 7   | 1   | 2   |
| 10  | 11  | 12  | 13  | 14  | 8   | 9   |
| 17  | 18  | 19  | 20  | 21  | 15  | 16  |
| 24  | 25  | 26  | 27  | 28  | 22  | 23  |

**May**

| Sun | Mon | Tue | Wed | Thu | Fri | Sat |
|-----|-----|-----|-----|-----|-----|-----|
|     |     |     | 1   | 2   | 3   | 4   |
| 5   | 6   | 7   | 8   | 9   | 10  | 11  |
| 12  | 13  | 14  | 15  | 16  | 17  | 18  |
| 19  | 20  | 21  | 22  | 23  | 24  | 25  |
| 26  | 27  | 28  | 29  | 30  | 31  |     |

**July**

| Sun | Mon | Tue | Wed | Thu | Fri | Sat |
|-----|-----|-----|-----|-----|-----|-----|
|     | 1   | 2   | 3   | 4   | 5   | 6   |
| 7   | 8   | 9   | 10  | 11  | 12  | 13  |
| 14  | 15  | 16  | 17  | 18  | 19  | 20  |
| 21  | 22  | 23  | 24  | 25  | 26  | 27  |
| 28  | 29  | 30  | 31  |     |     |     |

**September**

| Sun | Mon | Tue | Wed | Thu | Fri | Sat |
|-----|-----|-----|-----|-----|-----|-----|
| 1   | 2   | 3   | 4   | 5   | 6   | 7   |
| 8   | 9   | 10  | 11  | 12  | 13  | 14  |
| 15  | 16  | 17  | 18  | 19  | 20  | 21  |
| 22  | 23  | 24  | 25  | 26  | 27  | 28  |
| 29  | 30  |     |     |     |     |     |

**November**

| Sun | Mon | Tue | Wed | Thu | Fri | Sat |
|-----|-----|-----|-----|-----|-----|-----|
| 3   | 4   | 5   | 6   | 7   | 1   | 2   |
| 10  | 11  | 12  | 13  | 14  | 8   | 9   |
| 17  | 18  | 19  | 20  | 21  | 15  | 16  |
| 24  | 25  | 26  | 27  | 28  | 22  | 23  |
|     |     |     |     |     | 29  | 30  |

# INTEGRATED CIVICS UNIT CHECKUP

**How well did you learn the content in this unit?**
**Fill in the circle in front of the correct answer.**

1. Which is a U.S. territory now?
   - ○ Puerto Rico
   - ○ Louisiana
   - ○ Oregon
   - ○ Washington, D.C.

2. Where is the Statue of Liberty?
   - ○ Washington, D.C.
   - ○ Missouri River
   - ○ New York Harbor
   - ○ Philadelphia

3. What are the two longest rivers in the United States?
   - ○ Missouri and Colorado
   - ○ Mississippi and Connecticut
   - ○ Ohio and Rio Grande
   - ○ Mississippi and Missouri

4. Who lived in America before the Europeans arrived?
   - ○ Native Americans/American Indians
   - ○ Pilgrims
   - ○ Colonists
   - ○ Christopher Columbus

5. Who was Martin Luther King, Jr. ?
   - ○ A Republican leader
   - ○ A Pilgrim leader
   - ○ A civil rights leader
   - ○ A governor

6. What is the name of the national anthem?
   - ○ The Constitution
   - ○ The Bill of Rights
   - ○ The "Star-Spangled Banner"
   - ○ The Declaration of Independence

7. What do we show loyalty to when we say the Pledge of Allegiance?
   - ○ The Constitution
   - ○ Our state
   - ○ The President
   - ○ The United States of America

8. Why are there thirteen stripes on the flag?
   - ○ One for each state
   - ○ One for each amendment to the Constitution
   - ○ One for each Cabinet member
   - ○ One for each of the first 13 states

9. Why did the Pilgrims come to America?
   - ○ To meet Native Americans/ American Indians
   - ○ To find gold
   - ○ To gain religious freedom
   - ○ To celebrate Thanksgiving

10. Which state borders Canada?
    - ○ Minnesota
    - ○ Indiana
    - ○ Texas
    - ○ South Dakota

**11.** Independence Day celebrates independence from what country?
- ○ France
- ○ England
- ○ Germany
- ○ Japan

**12.** Why are there 50 stars on the flag?
- ○ One for each President
- ○ One for each amendment to the Constitution
- ○ They just look nice.
- ○ One for each state

**13.** Which state borders Mexico?
- ○ Montana
- ○ Colorado
- ○ Florida
- ○ California

**14.** What do we celebrate on the Fourth of July ?
- ○ Flag Day
- ○ Independence Day
- ○ President's Day
- ○ Veteran's Day

**15.** What holiday was celebrated for the first time by the American colonists?
- ○ Independence Day
- ○ Memorial Day
- ○ Thanksgiving
- ○ Labor Day

**16.** What is the date of Independence Day?
- ○ January 1
- ○ July 1
- ○ July 4
- ○ The first Monday in September

# TALK ABOUT IT

**Talk about what you learned in this unit. Work with a partner.**
**What would you like to learn more about? Make a list.**

_____

_____

_____

_____

_____

_____

**Share one idea with the class.**

# ABOUT THE BILL OF RIGHTS

**The Bill of Rights is the first ten amendments to the Constitution. The Bill of Rights guarantees the following:**

**Amendment 1**   Freedom of Religion, Speech, Press, Assembly, and Petition
- ★ People can practice any religion they want, or no religion at all.
- ★ People can say what they believe to be true.
- ★ People can write and print what they believe to be true.
- ★ People can meet in groups in a peaceful way and for peaceful reasons.
- ★ People can ask the government to change something they think is wrong.

**Amendment 2**   The Right to Bear Arms
- ★ People can own guns (with some restrictions).

**Amendment 3**   The Housing of Soldiers
- ★ The government cannot make people keep soldiers in their homes during peacetime.

**Amendment 4**   Search and Arrest
- ★ The government cannot search people's homes or arrest people without a warrant.

**Amendment 5**   The Rights of Accused Persons
- ★ People cannot be tried twice for the same crime. They also have the right to refuse to testify against themselves.

**Amendment 6**   The Right to a Fair Trial
- ★ People accused of a crime have the right to a speedy, public, and fair trial. They also have the right to a lawyer.

**Amendment 7**   Civil Cases
- ★ People have the right to a jury trial in most civil cases.

**Amendment 8**   Bail and Punishment
- ★ People cannot be asked to pay very high fines or be given cruel or unusual punishment.

**Amendment 9**   Other Rights
- ★ People have rights not listed in the Constitution. These rights must be protected by the government.

**Amendment 10**   Powers Belonging to States
- ★ Any powers that the Constitution did not give to the federal government belong to the state governments or to the people.

# THE STAR-SPANGLED BANNER

**The "Star-Spangled Banner" is the national anthem of the United States of America.**
**The lyrics were written by Francis Scott Key in 1814.**

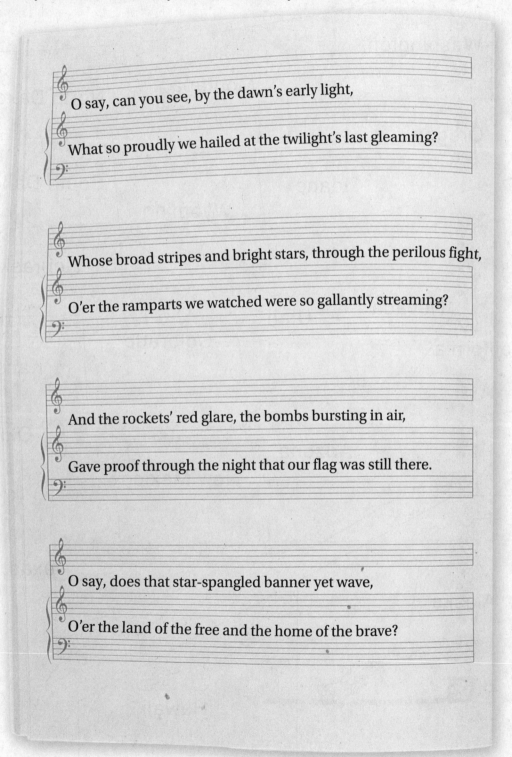

O say, can you see, by the dawn's early light,

What so proudly we hailed at the twilight's last gleaming?

Whose broad stripes and bright stars, through the perilous fight,

O'er the ramparts we watched were so gallantly streaming?

And the rockets' red glare, the bombs bursting in air,

Gave proof through the night that our flag was still there.

O say, does that star-spangled banner yet wave,

O'er the land of the free and the home of the brave?

# THE UNITED STATES OF AMERICA

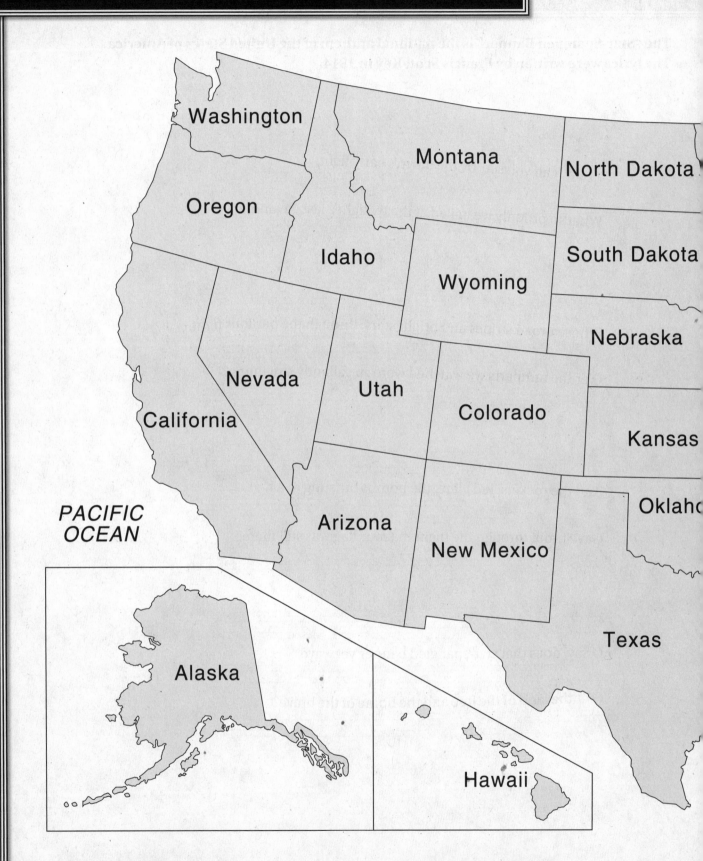

Washington

Montana

North Dakota

Oregon

South Dakota

Idaho

Wyoming

Nebraska

Nevada

Utah

Colorado

California

Kansas

PACIFIC
OCEAN

Arizona

Oklaho

New Mexico

Texas

Alaska

Hawaii

esota

Wisconsin

Michigan

wa

Illinois

Missouri

Indiana

Ohio

West
Virginia

Kentucky

rkansas

Tennesee

Mississippi

Alabama

Louisiana

Vermont

Maine

New Hampshire
Massachusetts

New York

Pennsylvania

Rhode Island
Connecticut

New Jersey

Delaware
Maryland

Virginia

North Carolina

South Carolina

Georgia

Florida

ATLANTIC
OCEAN

N

W   E

S

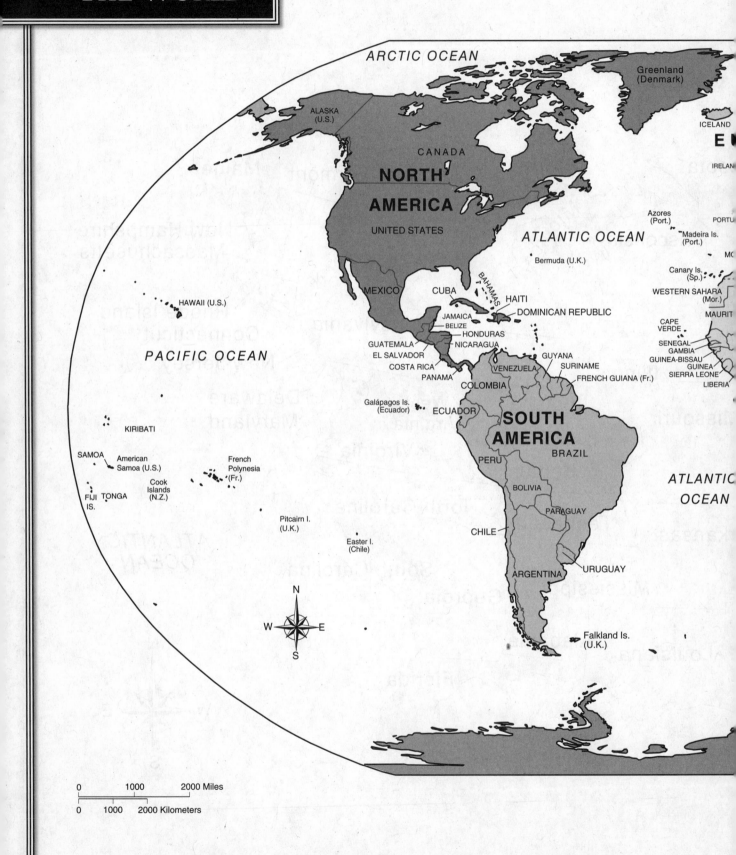

ARCTIC OCEAN

Greenland
(Denmark)

ICELAND

E U

IRELAND

ALASKA
(U.S.)

CANADA

NORTH
AMERICA

UNITED STATES

ATLANTIC OCEAN

Azores
(Port.)

PORTU

Madeira Is.
(Port.)

MO

Bermuda (U.K.)

Canary Is.
(Sp.)

HAWAII (U.S.)

WESTERN SAHARA
(Mor.)

MAURIT

MEXICO

CUBA

HAITI

CAPE
VERDE

DOMINICAN REPUBLIC

JAMAICA

BAHAMAS

SENEGAL
GAMBIA

PACIFIC OCEAN

BELIZE

HONDURAS

GUATEMALA

GUINEA-BISSAU

NICARAGUA

EL SALVADOR

GUYANA

GUINEA

COSTA RICA

VENEZUELA

SURINAME

SIERRA LEONE

PANAMA

FRENCH GUIANA (Fr.)

LIBERIA

COLOMBIA

Galápagos Is.
(Ecuador)

ECUADOR

SOUTH
AMERICA

KIRIBATI

BRAZIL

ATLANTIC

PERU

SAMOA

American
Samoa (U.S.)

French
Polynesia
(Fr.)

OCEAN

Cook
Islands
(N.Z.)

BOLIVIA

FIJI
IS.

TONGA

PARAGUAY

Pitcairn I.
(U.K.)

CHILE

Easter I.
(Chile)

N

W E

S

ARGENTINA

URUGUAY

Falkland Is.
(U.K.)

| 0 | 1000 | 2000 Miles |
| 0 | 1000 | 2000 Kilometers |

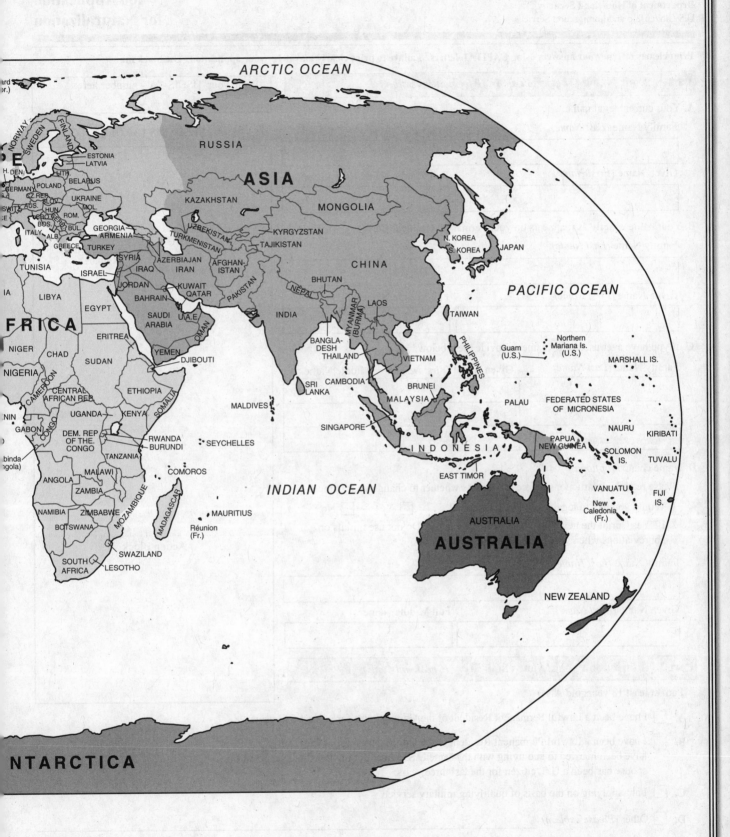

**Department of Homeland Security**
U.S Citizenship and Immigration Services

# N-400 Application
# for Naturalization

Print clearly or type your answers using CAPITAL letters. Failure to print clearly may delay your application. Use black ink.

## Part 1. Your Name. *(The person applying for naturalization.)*

Write your USCIS "A"- number here:
A

**A.** Your current legal name.

Family Name *(Last Name)*

Given Name *(First Name)*   Full Middle Name *(If applicable)*

**For USCIS Use Only**

| Bar Code | Date Stamp |
|---|---|

**B.** Your name **exactly** as it appears on your Permanent Resident Card.

Family Name *(Last Name)*

Given Name *(First Name)*   Full Middle Name *(If applicable)*

Remarks

**C.** If you have ever used other names, provide them below.

| Family Name *(Last Name)* | Given Name *(First Name)* | Middle Name |
|---|---|---|
|  |  |  |
|  |  |  |
|  |  |  |

**D.** Name change *(optional)*

Please read the Instructions before you decide whether to change your name.

**1.** Would you like to legally change your name?   ☐ Yes   ☐ No

**2.** If "Yes," print the new name you would like to use. Do not use initials or abbreviations when writing your new name.

Action Block

Family Name *(Last Name)*

Given Name *(First Name)*   Full Middle Name

## Part 2. Information about your eligibility. *(Check only one.)*

I am at least 18 years old **AND**

**A.** ☐ I have been a Lawful Permanent Resident of the United States for at least five years.

**B.** ☐ I have been a Lawful Permanent Resident of the United States for at least three years, **and** I have been married to and living with the same U.S. citizen for the last three years, **and** my spouse has been a U.S. citizen for the last three years.

**C.** ☐ I am applying on the basis of qualifying military service.

**D.** ☐ Other *(Please explain)*

Write your USCIS "A"- number here:
A

**A.** U.S. Social Security Number

**B.** Date of Birth *(mm/dd/yyyy)*

**C.** Date You Became a Permanent Resident *(mm/dd/yyyy)*

**D.** Country of Birth

**E.** Country of Nationality

F. Are either of your parents U.S. citizens? *(If yes, see instructions.)*  ☐ Yes  ☐ No

**G.** What is your current marital status?  ☐ Single, Never Married  ☐ Married  ☐ Divorced  ☐ Widowed

☐ Marriage Annulled or Other *(Explain)* _____

**H.** Are you requesting a waiver of the English and/or U.S. History and Government requirements based on a disability or impairment and attaching a Form N-648 with your application?  ☐ Yes  ☐ No

**I.** Are you requesting an accommodation to the naturalization process because of a disability or impairment? *(See Instructions for some examples of accommodations.)*  ☐ Yes  ☐ No

If you answered "Yes," check the box below that applies:

☐ I am deaf or hearing impaired and need a sign language interpreter who uses the following language: _____

☐ I use a wheelchair.

☐ I am blind or sight impaired.

☐ I will need another type of accommodation. Please explain: _____

_____

Part 4. **Addresses and telephone numbers.**

**A.** Home Address - Street Number and Name *(Do **not** write a P.O. Box in this space.)*   Apartment Number

City   County   State   ZIP Code   Country

**B.** Care of   Mailing Address - Street Number and Name *(If different from home address)*   Apartment Number

City   State   ZIP Code   Country

**C.** Daytime Phone Number *(If any)*   Evening Phone Number *(If any)*   E-mail Address *(If any)*

( )   ( )

## Part 5. Information for criminal records search.

**NOTE:** The categories below are those required by the FBI. See Instructions for more information.

**A.** Gender

☐ Male ☐ Female

**B.** Height

| Feet | Inches |

**C.** Weight

| Pounds |

**D.** Are you Hispanic or Latino? ☐ Yes ☐ No

**E.** Race *(Select one or more.)*

☐ White ☐ Asian ☐ Black or African American ☐ American Indian or Alaskan Native ☐ Native Hawaiian or Other Pacific Islander

**F.** Hair color

☐ Black ☐ Brown ☐ Blonde ☐ Gray ☐ White ☐ Red ☐ Sandy ☐ Bald (No Hair)

**G.** Eye color

☐ Brown ☐ Blue ☐ Green ☐ Hazel ☐ Gray ☐ Black ☐ Pink ☐ Maroon ☐ Other

## Part 6. Information about your residence and employment.

**A.** Where have you lived during the last five years? Begin with where you live now and then list every place you lived for the last five years. If you need more space, use a separate sheet(s) of paper.

| Street Number and Name, Apartment Number, City, State, Zip Code and Country | Dates *(mm/dd/yyyy)* | |
|---|---|---|
| | From | To |
| Current Home Address - Same as Part 4.A | | Present |
| | | |
| | | |
| | | |
| | | |

**B.** Where have you worked (or, if you were a student, what schools did you attend) during the last five years? Include military service. Begin with your current or latest employer and then list every place you have worked or studied for the last five years. If you need more space, use a separate sheet of paper.

| Employer or School Name | Employer or School Address *(Street, City and State)* | Dates *(mm/dd/yyyy)* | | Your Occupation |
|---|---|---|---|---|
| | | From | To | |
| | | | | |
| | | | | |
| | | | | |
| | | | | |
| | | | | |

## Part 7. Time outside the United States.
*(Including Trips to Canada, Mexico and the Caribbean Islands)*

**A.** How many total days did you spend outside of the United States during the past five years? [        ] days

**B.** How many trips of 24 hours or more have you taken outside of the United States during the past five years? [        ] trips

**C.** List below all the trips of 24 hours or more that you have taken outside of the United States since becoming a Lawful Permanent Resident. Begin with your most recent trip. If you need more space, use a separate sheet(s) of paper.

| Date You Left the United States *(mm/dd/yyyy)* | Date You Returned to the United States *(mm/dd/yyyy)* | Did Trip Last Six Months or More? | Countries to Which You Traveled | Total Days Out of the United States |
|---|---|---|---|---|
| | | ☐ Yes ☐ No | | |
| | | ☐ Yes ☐ No | | |
| | | ☐ Yes ☐ No | | |
| | | ☐ Yes ☐ No | | |
| | | ☐ Yes ☐ No | | |
| | | ☐ Yes ☐ No | | |
| | | ☐ Yes ☐ No | | |
| | | ☐ Yes ☐ No | | |
| | | ☐ Yes ☐ No | | |
| | | ☐ Yes ☐ No | | |

## Part 8. Information about your marital history.

**A.** How many times have you been married (including annulled marriages)? [        ] If you have **never** been married, go to Part 9.

**B.** If you are now married, give the following information about your spouse:

**1.** Spouse's Family Name *(Last Name)*    Given Name *(First Name)*    Full Middle Name *(If applicable)*

[                    ]    [                    ]    [                    ]

**2.** Date of Birth *(mm/dd/yyyy)*    **3.** Date of Marriage *(mm/dd/yyyy)*    **4.** Spouse's U.S. Social Security #

[                    ]    [                    ]    [                    ]

**5.** Home Address - Street Number and Name    Apartment Number

[                    ]    [                    ]

City    State    Zip Code

[                    ]    [                    ]    [                    ]

Write your USCIS "A"- number here:
A

**C.** Is your spouse a U.S. citizen? ☐ Yes ☐ No

**D.** If your spouse is a U.S. citizen, give the following information:

1. When did your spouse become a U.S. citizen? ☐ At Birth ☐ Other

   If "Other," give the following information:

   **2.** Date your spouse became a U.S. citizen

   **3.** Place your spouse became a U.S. citizen *(Please see Instructions.)*

   City and State

**E.** If your spouse is **not** a U.S. citizen, give the following information :

   **1.** Spouse's Country of Citizenship

   **2.** Spouse's USCIS "A"- Number *(If applicable)*

   A

   **3.** Spouse's Immigration Status

   ☐ Lawful Permanent Resident   ☐ Other _____

**F.** If you were married before, provide the following information about your prior spouse. If you have more than one previous marriage, use a separate sheet(s) of paper to provide the information requested in Questions 1-5 below.

   **1.** Prior Spouse's Family Name *(Last Name)*   Given Name *(First Name)*   Full Middle Name *(If applicable)*

   **2.** Prior Spouse's Immigration Status

   ☐ U.S. Citizen

   ☐ Lawful Permanent Resident

   ☐ Other _____

   **3.** Date of Marriage *(mm/dd/yyyy)*

   **4.** Date Marriage Ended *(mm/dd/yyyy)*

   **5.** How Marriage Ended

   ☐ Divorce   ☐ Spouse Died   ☐ Other

**G.** How many times has your current spouse been married (including annulled marriages)? ☐

   If your spouse has **ever** been married before, give the following information about **your spouse's** prior marriage.
   If your spouse has more than one previous marriage, use a separate sheet(s) of paper to provide the information requested in
   Questions 1 - 5 below.

   **1.** Prior Spouse's Family Name *(Last Name)*   Given Name *(First Name)*   Full Middle Name *(If applicable)*

   **2.** Prior Spouse's Immigration Status

   ☐ U.S. Citizen

   ☐ Lawful Permanent Resident

   ☐ Other _____

   **3.** Date of Marriage *(mm/dd/yyyy)*

   **4.** Date Marriage Ended *(mm/dd/yyyy)*

   **5.** How Marriage Ended

   ☐ Divorce   ☐ Spouse Died   ☐ Other

Write your USCIS "A"- number here:
A

**A.** How many sons and daughters have you had? For more information on which sons and daughters you should include and how to complete this section, see the Instructions.

**B.** Provide the following information about all of your sons and daughters. If you need more space, use a separate sheet(s) of paper.

| Full Name of Son or Daughter | Date of Birth (mm/dd/yyyy) | USCIS "A"- number (if child has one) | Country of Birth | Current Address (Street, City, State and Country) |
|---|---|---|---|---|
| | | A | | |
| | | A | | |
| | | A | | |
| | | A | | |
| | | A | | |
| | | A | | |
| | | A | | |
| | | A | | |

Add Children

Go to continuation page

**Part 10. Additional questions.**

Please answer Questions 1 through 14. If you answer "Yes" to any of these questions, include a written explanation with this form. Your written explanation should (1) explain why your answer was "Yes" and (2) provide any additional information that helps to explain your answer.

**A. General Questions.**

1. Have you **ever** claimed to be a U.S. citizen *(in writing or any other way)*? ☐ Yes ☐ No

2. Have you **ever** registered to vote in any Federal, state or local election in the United States? ☐ Yes ☐ No

3. Have you **ever** voted in any Federal, state or local election in the United States? ☐ Yes ☐ No

4. Since becoming a Lawful Permanent Resident, have you **ever** failed to file a required Federal state or local tax return? ☐ Yes ☐ No

5. Do you owe any Federal, state or local taxes that are overdue? ☐ Yes ☐ No

6. Do you have any title of nobility in any foreign country? ☐ Yes ☐ No

7. Have you ever been declared legally incompetent or been confined to a mental institution within the last five years? ☐ Yes ☐ No

## B.  Affiliations.

**8. a**  Have you **ever** been a member of or associated with any organization, association, fund foundation, party, club, society or similar group in the United States or in any other place?   ☐ Yes   ☐ No

**b.** If you answered "Yes," list the name of each group below. If you need more space, attach the names of the other group(s) on a separate sheet(s) of paper.

| Name of Group | Name of Group |
|---|---|
| **1.** | **6.** |
| **2.** | **7.** |
| **3.** | **8.** |
| **4.** | **9.** |
| **5.** | **10.** |

**9.**  Have you **ever** been a member of or in any way associated *(either directly or indirectly)* with:

  **a.**  The Communist Party?   ☐ Yes   ☐ No

  **b.**  Any other totalitarian party?   ☐ Yes   ☐ No

  **c**.  A terrorist organization?   ☐ Yes   ☐ No

**10.**  Have you **ever** advocated *(either directly or indirectly)* the overthrow of any government by force or violence?   ☐ Yes   ☐ No

**11.**  Have you **ever** persecuted *(either directly or indirectly)* any person because of race, religion, national origin, membership in a particular social group or political opinion?   ☐ Yes   ☐ No

**12.**  Between March 23, 1933 and May 8, 1945, did you work for or associate in any way *(either directly or indirectly)* with:

  **a.**  The Nazi government of Germany?   ☐ Yes   ☐ No

  **b.**  Any government in any area (1) occupied by, (2) allied with, or (3) established with the help of the Nazi government of Germany?   ☐ Yes   ☐ No

  **c.**  Any German, Nazi, or S.S. military unit, paramilitary unit, self-defense unit, vigilante unit, citizen unit, police unit, government agency or office, extermination camp, concentration camp, prisoner of war camp, prison, labor camp or transit camp?   ☐ Yes   ☐ No

## C.  Continuous Residence.

Since becoming a Lawful Permanent Resident of the United States:

**13.**  Have you **ever** called yourself a "nonresident" on a Federal, state or local tax return?   ☐ Yes   ☐ No

**14.**  Have you **ever** failed to file a Federal, state or local tax return because you considered yourself to be a "nonresident"?   ☐ Yes   ☐ No

Write your USCIS "A"- number here:
A

## D. Good Moral Character.

For the purposes of this application, you must answer "Yes" to the following questions, if applicable, even if your records were sealed or otherwise cleared or if anyone, including a judge, law enforcement officer or attorney, told you that you no longer have a record.

15. Have you **ever** committed a crime or offense for which you were **not** arrested? ☐ Yes ☐ No

16. Have you **ever** been arrested, cited or detained by any law enforcement officer (including USCIS or former INS and military officers) for any reason? ☐ Yes ☐ No

17. Have you **ever** been charged with committing any crime or offense? ☐ Yes ☐ No

18. Have you **ever** been convicted of a crime or offense? ☐ Yes ☐ No

19. Have you **ever** been placed in an alternative sentencing or a rehabilitative program (for example: diversion, deferred prosecution, withheld adjudication, deferred adjudication)? ☐ Yes ☐ No

20. Have you **ever** received a suspended sentence, been placed on probation or been paroled? ☐ Yes ☐ No

21. Have you **ever** been in jail or prison? ☐ Yes ☐ No

If you answered "Yes" to any of Questions 15 through 21, complete the following table. If you need more space, use a separate sheet (s) of paper to give the same information.

| Why were you arrested, cited, detained or charged? | Date arrested, cited, detained or charged? *(mm/dd/yyyy)* | Where were you arrested, cited, detained or charged? *(City, State, Country)* | Outcome or disposition of the arrest, citation, detention or charge *(No charges filed, charges dismissed, jail, probation, etc.)* |
|---|---|---|---|
| | | | |
| | | | |
| | | | |

Answer Questions 22 through 33. If you answer "Yes" to any of these questions, attach (1) your written explanation why your answer was "Yes" and (2) any additional information or documentation that helps explain your answer.

22. Have you **ever**:

   **a.** Been a habitual drunkard? ☐ Yes ☐ No

   **b.** Been a prostitute, or procured anyone for prostitution? ☐ Yes ☐ No

   **c.** Sold or smuggled controlled substances, illegal drugs or narcotics? ☐ Yes ☐ No

   **d.** Been married to more than one person at the same time? ☐ Yes ☐ No

   **e.** Helped anyone enter or try to enter the United States illegally? ☐ Yes ☐ No

   **f.** Gambled illegally or received income from illegal gambling? ☐ Yes ☐ No

   **g.** Failed to support your dependents or to pay alimony? ☐ Yes ☐ No

23. Have you **ever** given false or misleading information to any U.S. government official while applying for any immigration benefit or to prevent deportation, exclusion or removal? ☐ Yes ☐ No

24. Have you **ever** lied to any U.S. government official to gain entry or admission into the United States? ☐ Yes ☐ No

### E. Removal, Exclusion and Deportation Proceedings.

**25.** Are removal, exclusion, rescission or deportation proceedings pending against you?   ☐ Yes   ☐ No

**26.** Have you **ever** been removed, excluded or deported from the United States?   ☐ Yes   ☐ No

**27.** Have you **ever** been ordered to be removed, excluded or deported from the United States?   ☐ Yes   ☐ No

**28.** Have you **ever** applied for any kind of relief from removal, exclusion or deportation?   ☐ Yes   ☐ No

### F. Military Service.

**29.** Have you **ever** served in the U.S. Armed Forces?   ☐ Yes   ☐ No

**30.** Have you **ever** left the United States to avoid being drafted into the U.S. Armed Forces?   ☐ Yes   ☐ No

**31.** Have you **ever** applied for any kind of exemption from military service in the U.S. Armed Forces?   ☐ Yes   ☐ No

**32.** Have you **ever** deserted from the U.S. Armed Forces?   ☐ Yes   ☐ No

### G. Selective Service Registration.

**33.** Are you a male who lived in the United States at any time between your 18th and 26th birthdays in any status except as a lawful nonimmigrant?   ☐ Yes   ☐ No

If you answered "NO," go on to question 34.

If you answered "YES," provide the information below.

If you answered "YES," but you did not register with the Selective Service System and are still under 26 years of age, you must register before you apply for naturalization, so that you can complete the information below:

Date Registered (mm/dd/yyyy) [          ]   Selective Service Number [          ]

If you answered "YES," but you did not register with the Selective Service and you are now 26 years old or older, attach a statement explaining why you did not register.

### H. Oath Requirements. *(See Part 14 for the Text of the Oath.)*

Answer Questions 34 through 39. If you answer "No" to any of these questions, attach (1) your written explanation why the answer was "No" and (2) any additional information or documentation that helps to explain your answer.

**34.** Do you support the Constitution and form of government of the United States?   ☐ Yes   ☐ No

**35.** Do you understand the full Oath of Allegiance to the United States?   ☐ Yes   ☐ No

**36.** Are you willing to take the full Oath of Allegiance to the United States?   ☐ Yes   ☐ No

**37.** If the law requires it, are you willing to bear arms on behalf of the United States?   ☐ Yes   ☐ No

**38.** If the law requires it, are you willing to perform noncombatant services in the U.S. Armed Forces?   ☐ Yes   ☐ No

**39.** If the law requires it, are you willing to perform work of national importance under civilian direction?   ☐ Yes   ☐ No

Form N-400 (Rev. 10/15/07) Y Page 9

.Write your USCIS "A"- number here:
A

I certify, under penalty of perjury under the laws of the United States of America, that this application, and the evidence submitted with it, are all true and correct. I authorize the release of any information that the USCIS needs to determine my eligibility for naturalization.

Your Signature

Date *(mm/dd/yyyy)*

## Part 12. Signature of person who prepared this application for you. *(If applicable.)*

I declare under penalty of perjury that I prepared this application at the request of the above person. The answers provided are based on information of which I have personal knowledge and/or were provided to me by the above named person in response to the *exact questions* contained on this form.

Preparer's Printed Name

Preparer's Signature

Date *(mm/dd/yyyy)*

Preparer's Firm or Organization Name *(If applicable)*

Preparer's Daytime Phone Number

Preparer's Address - Street Number and Name

City

State

Zip Code

### NOTE: Do not complete Parts 13 and 14 until a USCIS Officer instructs you to do so.

## Part 13. Signature at interview.

I swear (affirm) and certify under penalty of perjury under the laws of the United States of America that I know that the contents of this application for naturalization subscribed by me, including corrections numbered 1 through _____ and the evidence submitted by me numbered pages 1 through _____, are true and correct to the best of my knowledge and belief.

Subscribed to and sworn to (affirmed) before me

Officer's Printed Name or Stamp

Date *(mm/dd/yyyy)*

Complete Signature of Applicant

Officer's Signature

## Part 14. Oath of Allegiance.

If your application is approved, you will be scheduled for a public oath ceremony at which time you will be required to take the following oath of allegiance immediately prior to becoming a naturalized citizen. By signing, you acknowledge your willingness and ability to take this oath:

I hereby declare, on oath, that I absolutely and entirely renounce and abjure all allegiance and fidelity to any foreign prince, potentate, state, or sovereignty, of whom or which I have heretofore been a subject or citizen;

that I will support and defend the Constitution and laws of the United States of America against all enemies, foreign and domestic;

that I will bear true faith and allegiance to the same;

that I will bear arms on behalf of the United States when required by the law;

that I will perform noncombatant service in the Armed Forces of the United States when required by the law;

that I will perform work of national importance under civilian direction when required by the law; and

that I take this obligation freely, without any mental reservation or purpose of evasion; so help me God.

Printed Name of Applicant

Complete Signature of Applicant

# CITIZENSHIP QUESTIONS AND ANSWERS

To be eligible for naturalization, you have to be able to read, write, and speak basic English. You must also have a basic knowledge of U.S. history and government. The questions on the next five pages are examples of questions a USCIS officer may ask you at your interview.

Track 15

## Unit 1: U.S. History

1. What is the supreme law of the land?
2. What does the Constitution do?

3. The idea of self-government is in the first three words of the Constitution. What are these words?

4. What is an amendment?
5. What do we call the first ten amendments to the Constitution?
6. What is <u>one</u> right or freedom from the First Amendment?


7. How many amendments does the Constitution have?
8. What did the Declaration of Independence do?

9. What are <u>two</u> rights in the Declaration of Independence?
10. What is freedom of religion?

11. There are four amendments to the Constitution about who can vote. Describe <u>one</u> of them.

12. What is <u>one</u> responsibility that is only for United States citizens?
13. What are <u>two</u> rights only for United States citizens?
14. What are <u>two</u> rights of everyone living in the United States?


1. The Constitution
2. It sets up the government and protects the basic rights of Americans.
3. We the People


4. A change to the Constitution
5. The Bill of Rights
6. The rights of freedom:
   • of speech,
   • of religion,
   • of assembly,
   • of the press, and
   • to petition the government


7. 27
8. Announced our independence from Great Britain
9. Life, liberty, and the pursuit of happiness
10. You can practice any religion, or not practice a religion.
11. Citizens 18 and older can vote, you don't have to pay a tax to vote, both women and men can vote, or a citizen of any race can vote.
12. Serve on a jury, or vote
13. Apply for a federal job, vote, run for office, or carry a U.S. passport
14. Freedom of expression, freedom of speech, freedom of assembly, freedom to petition the government, or freedom of religion

**15.** What is <u>one</u> promise you make when you become a United States citizen?

**16.** When is the last day you can send in federal income tax forms?

**17.** When must all men register for the Selective Service?

**18.** What is <u>one</u> reason colonists came to America?

**19.** What group of people was taken to America and sold as slaves?

**20.** Why did the colonists fight the British?

**21.** Who wrote the Declaration of Independence?

**22.** When was the Declaration of Independence adopted?

**23.** There were 13 original states. Name <u>three</u>.

**24.** What happened at the Constitutional Convention?

**25.** When was the Constitution written?

**26.** The Federalist Papers supported the passage of the U.S. Constitution. Name <u>one</u> of the writers.

**27.** What is <u>one</u> thing Benjamin Franklin is famous for?

**28.** Who is the "Father of Our Country"?

**29.** Who was the first President?

**30.** Name <u>one</u> war fought by the United States in the 1800s.

**31.** Name the U.S. war between the North and the South.

**32.** Name <u>one</u> problem that led to the Civil War.

**33.** What was <u>one</u> important thing that Abraham Lincoln did?

**34.** What did the Emancipation Proclamation do?

**15.** Give up loyalty to other countries, obey the laws of the United States, serve the country, and be loyal to the United States

**16.** April 15

**17.** At age 18, or between 18 and 26

**18.** Political freedom, religious freedom, or to escape persecution

**19.** Africans

**20.** Because of high taxes, because the British army stayed in their houses, or because they didn't have self-government

**21.** Thomas Jefferson

**22.** July 4, 1776

**23.** New Hampshire, Massachusetts, Rhode Island, Connecticut, New York, New Jersey, Pennsylvania, Delaware, Maryland, Virginia, North Carolina, South Carolina, and Georgia

**24.** The Constitution was written

**25.** 1787

**26.** James Madison, Alexander Hamilton, or John Jay

**27.** U.S. diplomat, oldest member of the Constitutional Convention, first Postmaster General of the United States, or started the first free libraries

**28.** George Washington

**29.** George Washington

**30.** The War of 1812, the Mexican-American War, the Civil War, or the Spanish-American War

**31.** The Civil War

**32.** Slavery, economic reasons, or states' rights

**33.** Freed the slaves, saved the Union, or led the United States during the Civil War

**34.** Freed the slaves

## Unit 1: U.S. History *continued*

**35.** What did Susan B. Anthony do?

**36.** Name <u>one</u> war fought by the United States in the 1900s.

**37.** Who was President during World War I?

**38.** Who was President during the Great Depression and World War II?

**39.** Who did the United States fight in World War II?

**40.** Before he was President, Eisenhower was a general. What war was he in?

**41.** During the Cold War, what was the main concern of the United States?

**42.** What major event happened on September 11, 2001, in the United States?

**35.** Fought for women's rights

**36.** World War I, World War II, the Korean War, the Vietnam War, or the Persian Gulf War

**37.** Woodrow Wilson

**38.** Franklin Roosevelt

**39.** Japan, Germany, and Italy

**40.** World War II

**41.** Communism

**42.** Terrorists attacked the United States.

Track 16

## Unit 2: U.S. Government

**1.** What is the economic system in the United States?

**2.** What is the "rule of law"?

**3.** Name <u>one</u> branch or part of the government.

**4.** What stops <u>one</u> branch of government from becoming too powerful?

**5.** Who is in charge of the executive branch?

**6.** Who makes federal laws?

**7.** What are the <u>two</u> parts of the U.S. Congress?

**8.** How many U.S. senators are there?

**9.** We elect a U.S. senator for how many years?

**10.** Who is <u>one</u> of your state's U.S. senators?

**11.** The House of Representatives has how many voting members?

**12.** We elect a U.S. representative for how many years?

**13.** Name your U.S. representative.

**14.** Who does a U.S. senator represent?

**15.** Why do some states have more Representatives than other states?

**16.** We elect a President for how many years?

**17.** In what month do we vote for President?

**18.** What is the name of the President of the United States now?

**1.** Capitalist, or market economy

**2.** Everyone must follow the law.

**3.** Legislative, executive, or judicial

**4.** Checks and balances, or the separation of powers

**5.** The President

**6.** Congress

**7.** The Senate and the House of Representatives

**8.** 100

**9.** 6

**10.** _____

**11.** 435

**12.** 2

**13.** _____

**14.** All people of the state

**15.** Because they have more people

**16.** 4

**17.** November

**18.** Barack Obama

**19.** What is the name of the Vice President of the United States now?

**20.** If the President can no longer serve, who becomes President?

**21.** If both the President and the Vice President can no longer serve, who becomes President?

**22.** Who is the Commander in Chief of the military?

**23.** Who signs bills to become laws?

**24.** Who vetoes bills?

**25.** What does the President's Cabinet do?

**26.** What are <u>two</u> Cabinet-level positions?

**27.** What does the judicial branch do?

**28.** What is the highest court in the United States?

**29.** How many justices are on the Supreme Court?

**30.** Who is the Chief Justice of the United States?

**31.** Under our Constitution, some powers belong to the federal government. What is <u>one</u> power of the federal government?

**32.** Under our Constitution, some powers belong to the states. What is <u>one</u> power of the states?

**33.** Who is the Governor of your state?

**34.** What is the capital of your state?

**35.** What are the <u>two</u> major political parties in the United States?

**36.** What is the political party of the President now?

**37.** What is the name of the Speaker of the House of Representatives now?

**38.** What are <u>two</u> ways that Americans can participate in their democracy?

**39.** What is the capital of the United States?

**40.** How old do citizens have to be to vote for President?

---

**19.** Joe Biden

**20.** The Vice President

**21.** The Speaker of the House

**22.** The President

**23.** The President

**24.** The President

**25.** Advises the President

**26.** Secretary of Defense, Secretary of Education, Secretary of State, Secretary of Treasury, or Attorney General

**27.** Explains laws and decides if a law goes against the Constitution

**28.** The Supreme Court

**29.** 9

**30.** John Roberts

**31.** To print money, to declare war, to create an army, or to make treaties

**32.** Provide education, provide protection, provide safety, or give a driver's license

**33.** _____

**34.** _____

**35.** Democratic and Republican

**36.** Democratic

**37.** Nancy Pelosi

**38.** Vote, join a political party, help with a campaign, join a community group, or call senators and representatives

**39.** Washington, D.C.

**40.** 18 and older

## Unit 3: Integrated Civics

1. What territory did the United States buy from France in 1803?

2. Name one of the two longest rivers in the United States.

3. What ocean is on the West Coast of the United States?

4. What ocean is on the East Coast of the United States?

5. Name one U.S. territory.

6. Name one state that borders Canada.

7. Name one state that borders Mexico.

8. Where is the Statue of Liberty?

9. Why does the flag have 13 stripes?

10. Why does the flag have 50 stars?

11. What is the name of the national anthem?

12. When do we celebrate Independence Day?

13. Name two national U.S. holidays.

14. Name one American Indian tribe in the United States.

15. Who lived in America before the Europeans arrived?

16. What movement tried to end racial discrimination?

17. What did Martin Luther King, Jr., do?

18. What do we show loyalty to when we say the Pledge of Allegiance?

---

1. The Louisiana Territory

2. The Missouri River, or the Mississippi River

3. Pacific Ocean

4. Atlantic Ocean

5. Puerto Rico, U.S. Virgin Islands, American Samoa, Northern Mariana Islands, or Guam

6. Maine, New Hampshire, Vermont, New York, Michigan, Minnesota, North Dakota, Montana, Idaho, Washington, or Alaska

7. California, Arizona, New Mexico, or Texas

8. New York Harbor or Liberty Island

9. Because there were 13 original colonies

10. Because there is one star for each state

11. The Star-Spangled Banner

12. July 4

13. Martin Luther King, Jr., Day, Presidents' Day, Memorial Day, Independence Day, Labor Day, or Thanksgiving

14. Cherokee, Sioux, Crow, Navajo, or Hopi

15. Native Americans, or American Indians

16. Civil Rights Movement

17. Fought for civil rights and worked for equality for all Americans

18. The United States of America, or the flag

# SENTENCES FOR DICTATION AND READING

The sentences on the next two pages are examples of the types of sentences a USCIS officer may ask you to read aloud or write during your interview.

Citizens have the right to vote.

Congress passes laws in the United States.

George Washington was the first President.

I want to be an American citizen.

Many people come to America for freedom.

Our government is divided into three branches.

People vote for the President in November.

The Constitution is the supreme law of our land.

The House and Senate are parts of Congress.

The President is elected every 4 years.

The President signs bills to make them laws.

The capital of the United States is Washington, D.C.

The United States flag has thirteen stripes.

There are 50 stars on the flag.

Who is the Father of our country?

_____

The flag is red, white, and blue.

_____

Alaska is the largest state in the United States.

_____

How many Senators are in Congress?

_____

Independence Day is in July.

_____

Mexico is south of the United States.

_____

Citizens in the United States have the right to freedom of speech.

_____

The President lives in the White House.

_____

The Civil War was fought between the North and the South.

_____

When is Thanksgiving?

_____

# QUESTIONS AND ANSWERS FOR THE 65/20 EXCEPTION

**If you are 65 years old or older and have been a legal permanent resident of the United States for 20 or more years, you may study just these questions.**

1. What is <u>one</u> right or freedom from the First Amendment?

2. What is <u>one</u> responsibility that is only for United States citizens?

3. When is the last day you can send in federal income tax forms?

4. Who was the first President?

5. What was <u>one</u> important thing that Abraham Lincoln did?

6. Name <u>one</u> war fought by the United States in the 1900s.

7. What is the economic system in the United States?

8. Name <u>one</u> branch or part of the government.

9. What are the <u>two</u> parts of the U.S. Congress?

10. Who is <u>one</u> of your state's U.S. senators?

11. In what month do we vote for President?

12. What is the name of the President of the United States now?

13. What is the capital of your state?

14. What is the capital of the United States?

15. What are the <u>two</u> major political parties in the United States?

16. How old do citizens have to be to vote for President?

17. Where is the Statue of Liberty?

18. Why does the flag have 50 stars?

19. When do we celebrate Independence Day?

20. What did Martin Luther King, Jr., do?

---

1. The rights of freedom:
   - of speech,
   - of religion,
   - of assembly,
   - of the press, and
   - to petition the government

2. Serve on a jury, or vote

3. April 15

4. George Washington

5. Freed the slaves, saved the Union, or led the United States during the Civil War

6. World War I, World War II, the Korean War, the Vietnam War, or the Persian Gulf War

7. Capitalist, or market economy

8. Legislative, executive, or judicial

9. The Senate and the House of Representatives

10. _____

11. November

12. Barack Obama

13. _____

14. Washington, D.C.

15. Democratic and Republican

16. 18 and older

17. New York Harbor, or Liberty Island

18. Because there is one star for each state

19. July 4

20. Fought for civil rights, and worked for equality for all Americans

**After you pass the citizenship test, you say the Oath of Allegiance and become a citizen of the United States of America.**

I hereby declare, on oath;

that I absolutely and entirely renounce and abjure

all allegiance and fidelity to any foreign prince,

potentate, state, or sovereignty, of whom or which

I have heretofore been a subject or citizen;

that I will support and defend the Constitution and the

laws of the United States of America against all enemies,

foreign and domestic;

that I will bear true faith and allegiance to the same;

that I will bear arms on behalf of the United States when

required by the law;

that I will perform noncombatant service in the Armed

Forces of the United States when required by the law;

that I will perform work of national importance under

civilian direction when required by the law; and

that I take this obligation freely, without any mental

reservation or purpose of evasion; so help me God.

# ANSWER KEY

## Unit 1: U.S. History

### ★ Lesson 1 — Page 10
**Complete the dialogs.**
> Revolutionary War, colonies, George
>     Washington, President, Father
> Independence, England, Declaration,
>     Thomas Jefferson, equal

### ★ Lesson 2 — Page 18
**Complete the puzzle.**
**Across:**   1. Franklin   5. Constitution
  6. speech   7. vote
**Down:**   2. amendment   3. Rights   4. citizen

### ★ Lesson 3 — Page 22
**Complete the sentences.**
  1. slavery   2. Abraham Lincoln   3. Confederate
  4. Emancipation Proclamation   5. Union

**Complete the puzzle.**
**Across:**   2. Emancipation   4. united
**Down:**   1. divided   3. Civil   4. Union

### ★ Lesson 4 — Page 26
**Match.**
  1. g   2. d   3. a   4. h   5. b   6. c   7. e   8. f

**Write four complete sentences based on the matching.**
**Possible answers:**   1. Woodrow Wilson was the U.S. President during World War I.   2. The Great Depression was a hard time after World War I.   3. 1914 was when World War I began.   4. Dwight D. Eisenhower was a general during World War II.

### ★ Lesson 5 — Page 29
**Complete the sentences.**
  1. Korean   2. Vietnam   3. 1973
  4. Persian Gulf   5. terrorists

### U.S. History Checkup — Pages 30–33
1. 1776   2. Freedom of speech   3. For religious freedom   4. Abraham Lincoln   5. Self-government   6. Africans   7. George Washington   8. All people living in the United States   9. An amendment   10. Communism
11. Virginia, Massachusetts, Maryland, Rhode Island, Connecticut, New Hampshire, North Carolina, South Carolina, New York, New Jersey, Pennsylvania, Delaware, Georgia
12. Abraham Lincoln   13. Voting   14. The Constitution   15. States' rights   16. World War I   17. Liberty   18. The Bill of Rights
19. 27   20. England   21. September 11, 2001
22. George Washington   23. The Bill of Rights
24. 1787   25. The Cabinet   26. 18   27. It freed the slaves.   28. To be loyal to the United States
29. April 15   30. Thomas Jefferson   31. The Constitution   32. Germany, Italy, and Japan

## Unit 2: U.S. Government

★ **Lesson 6**                                      Page 39

**Complete the chart.**
**The House of Representatives**
1. 435
2. 2
**The Senate**
1. 100
2. 6

★ **Lesson 7**                                      Page 43

**Complete the chart.**
1. The Vice President   2. The President
3. The President   4. The Vice President
5. The President

**Complete the sentences.**
1. 4   2. Republican   3. November
4. Barack Obama   5. Joe Biden

★ **Lesson 8**                                      Page 47

**Complete the sentences.**
1. Supreme Court   2. John Roberts
3. Congress

**Complete the chart.**
1. Executive   2. Legislative   3. Judicial

★ **Lesson 9**                                      Page 49

**Complete the sentences.**
Check answers with your instructor.

**Circle your state and state capital.**   Page 50
Check the map with your instructor.

**Plan a trip.**                                    Page 51
1. Boston—Massachusetts   2. Albany—New
York   3. Columbus—Ohio   4. Springfield—
Illinois   5. Tallahassee—Florida
6. Baton Rouge—Louisiana   7. Austin—Texas
8. Santa Fe—New Mexico   9. Phoenix—
Arizona   10. Sacramento—California

★ **Lesson 10**                                     Page 54

**Complete the charts.**
Check charts with your instructor.

**Complete the chart.**                             Page 55
1. Federal Government   2. State Government,
Federal Government   3. Federal Government
4. State Government   5. Federal Government
6. Federal Government   7. State Government

**Complete the sentences.**
1. Executive, Legislative and Judicial.
2. Executive, Legislative and Judicial.

**Complete the chart.**                             Page 57
1. State Government   2. State Government
3. Federal Government   4. Federal
Government   5. Federal Government

**Complete the sentences.**
1. democracy
2. two
3. Republican
4. branches

**U.S. Government Checkup**      Pages 58–60
1. John Roberts   2. The Supreme Court
3. Executive, Judicial, Legislative   4. Everyone
must follow the law.   5. Provide schooling and
education   6. Because of the number of people
in the state   7. Secretary of State   8. November
9. Separation of powers   10. The President
11. All people of a state   12. Advises the
President   13. The Speaker of the House
of Representatives   14. The President
15. Congress   16. 9   17. Barack Obama
18. Reviews laws   19. The President, the
Cabinet, and the departments under the
Cabinet   20. Democratic and Republican
21. To give a driver's license   22. The President
23. 100   24. The Senate and the House of
Representatives   25. Congress   26. Democratic
27. 435   28. Judicial   29. 4 years   30. The Vice
President   31. Market economy
32. Washington, D.C.

## Unit 3: Integrated Civics

★ **Lesson 11**        **Page 67**

**Complete the sentences.**
1. West Coast   2. New York, Idaho   3. Atlantic
4. Louisiana   5. Guam   6. Cherokee, Hopi
7. Arizona, New Mexico   8. Mississippi

★ **Lesson 12**        **Page 70**

**Complete the puzzle.**
**Across:**   2. Native Americans   4. Pilgrims
5. freedom
**Down:**   1. meal   2. November   3. Mayflower

★ **Lesson 13**        **Page 75**

**Complete the puzzle.**
**Across:**   5. Declaration   6. parade
**Down:**   1. stripe   2. July   3. Banner   4. Union
**Complete the sentences.**
1. stripe   2. Union   3. Banner   4. July
5. parade   6. Declaration

★ **Lesson 14**        **Page 79**

**Circle the dates of these holidays.**
Martin Luther King, Jr. Day—January 21
President's Day—February 18
Memorial Day—May 27
Independence Day —July 4
Labor Day—September 2
Veteran's Day—November 11

**Integrated Civics Checkup**      **Pages 80–81**
1. Puerto Rico   2. New York Harbor
3. Mississippi and Missouri   4. Native Americans/American Indians   5. A civil rights leader   6. The "Star-Spangled Banner"
7. The United States of America   8. One for each of the first 13 states   9. To gain religious freedom   10. Minnesota   11. England
12. One for each state   13. California
14. Independence Day   15. Thanksgiving
16. July 4